BLACK DOG OPERA LIBRARY

Rigoletto

BLACK DOG OPERA LIBRARY

Rigoletto

GIUSEPPE VERDI
TEXT BY DANIEL S. BRINK

BLACK DOG
& LEVENTHAL
PUBLISHERS
NEW YORK

Published by
Black Dog & Leventhal Publishers, Inc.
151 West 19th Street
New York, NY 10011

Distributed by
Workman Publishing Company
708 Broadway
New York, NY 10003

Series editor: Jessica MacMurray
Original Series Design: Alleycat Design, Inc.
Layout: Dutton & Sherman Design

Book manufactured in Canada

ISBN: 1-57912-047-4

h g f e d c b a

FOREWORD

*R*igoletto is truly one of the greatest operas ever written. It has no heroes, no clearly defined villain—but the story is characterized by a gloomy tragedy that stems from selfless and misguided love. Well received from the very beginning, *Rigoletto* is a masterwork from the definitive opera composer.

You will hear the entire opera on the two compact discs included on the inside front and back covers of this book. As you explore the book, you will discover the story behind the opera and its creation, the life of the composer, biographies of the principal singers and conductor, and the opera's text—or libretto—both in Italian and English. Expert commentary has been added to the libretto to aid in your appreciation and to highlight key moments in the score.

Enjoy this book and enjoy the music.

OTHER TITLES IN THE SERIES:

PHOTOGRAPHY CREDITS

Hulton Getty/Liaison Agency: p. 18, p. 19, p. 26, p. 46, p. 48
UPI/Corbis Bettman: p. 22
Corbis: p. 12
Gamma Liaison: p. 24, p. 34-5
Jack Vartoogian: p. 15, p. 16. p. 20-1, p. 28, p. 31
Cover : Superstock

About the Author

*D*aniel S. Brink is the author of three other titles in the Black Dog Oper a Library: *La Traviata, Madama Butterfly* and *Tosca*. He is also the Artistic Advisor and Principal Coach/Accompanist for the Colorado Opera Festival, Artistic Director for the Company Singers, a development program for young operatic hopefuls and Artistic Director/Conductor of the Colorado Springs Choral Society small ensemble, MOSIAC. Mr. Brink is a lecturer in Music and principal accompanist at The Colorado College, and has performed extensively in the United States and Europe. He is a highly regarded director, recitalist, teacher, adjudicator and writer.

Tosca

⌒

Giuseppe Verdi's story is truly a rags-to-riches classic. His life was marked by terrible tragedy and struggle, crowned by the esteem of the entire world. Giuseppe Verdi was many things: consummate artist, politician, shrewd business man and in all things, a man of simple truth and integrity.

He was born the son of a peasant farmer/shop owner in the tiny northern Italian village of Le Roncole on October 10, 1813. The elder of two children, his younger sister was mentally retarded and died while still in her teens. Even as a small child, Verdi demonstrated a fascination with music. He is said to have followed a wandering fiddler around his home town for hours at a time and he would become so entranced by the sound of the organ at Sunday Mass that he would sometimes forget his duties as acolyte. Observing his interest, sometime before his eighth birthday his parents gave him an old decrepit spinet—a small harpsichord. This style of instrument had long since been supplanted in popularity by the piano, but it must have seemed the gift of a lifetime to the budding musician.

GIUSEPPE VERDI (1813-1901)

The nearest town of any size was Busseto. Verdi's father, Carlo, had business dealings with Antonio Barezzi, one of the leading citizens of that town, who owned and operated the city's general store and served as the president of the Philharmonic Society: an amateur orchestra that performed for local events and concertized throughout the region. Through this connection, Carlo Verdi arranged for his ten-year-old son to board with a cobbler in Busseto and pursue his general education with a local priest, Don Pietro Seletti and his musical education with the music director at the local cathedral, Ferdinando Provesi.

Young Giuseppe worked hard both as the cobbler's assistant and as a student, but he excelled in his musical studies. Every Sunday he would trek three miles to his hometown on foot to play the organ at his home parish. Under Barezzi's mentorship, he began composing marches and overtures to be performed by the Philharmonic Society and was offered the opportunity to conduct the orchestra from time to time. Eventually, at age sixteen, he moved into Barezzi's home and earned his keep by assisting in the management of the family's business as well as the city's musical affairs.

As his obvious talents flourished, it was decided the young Verdi should study at the Milan Conservatory, the center of musical study in Italy. Milan was also the home of the famous opera house, Teatro alla Scala, considered to be the center of European Opera to this day among European houses. So, with the financial backing of Barezzi and a local charitable foundation, the nineteen-year-old Verdi moved to Milan. His application to the famous conservatory was rejected. Though no reason was given, it was no doubt due to his age and lack of formal conservatory training to date. His talent was evident, but still raw. Years later, after his fame was established, the conserva-

LEO NUCCI (RIGOLETTO) AND JOAN SUTHERLAND (GILDA)

tory expressed an interest in changing its name to the Verdi Conservatory. Verdi refused the honor, saying "they didn't want me when I was young, they can't have me now that I'm old."

Undaunted, the young musician arranged instead to study privately with Vincenzo Lavigna, who had made a name for himself as a conductor at La Scala. It was the perfect arrangement for Verdi and, surrounded by the rich musical culture of Milan, his potential began to be realized.

Verdi had been in Milan only a year when his former teacher, Provesi died. The cathedral in Busseto was left without a maestro—Barezzi and the Philharmonic Society wanted to hire Verdi for the position, while those at the cathedral backed a second candidate. The situation became a heated debate, with most of Busseto's citizens firmly entrenched in support of one candidate over the other. The battle waged on over a three year period the battle until finally, with the help of government intervention, Verdi was chosen for the post.

LUCIANO PAVAROTTI (THE DUKE) AND ISOLA JONES (MADDALENA)

Meanwhile, Verdi's studies with Lavigna had been completed and he was presented with an opera libretto, *Oberto, Conte di San Bonifacio,* which he had begun to compose when he returned to Busseto to accept his post. Now gainfully employed, he married Barezzi's eldest daughter, Margherita. They had fallen in love during the time he had been living and working in Barezzi's home. He settled into life with his new job and new wife in Busseto while continuing to work on *Oberto* and maintaining his ties in Milan, hoping to see his first opera produced there. He had opportunity to be introduced to the new impresario at La Scala, Bartolomeo Merelli, and over a long period of negotiation and failed attempts was finally granted a production of *Oberto* in the autumn of 1839. The opera proved to be a huge success, prompting Merelli to commission three new works from the young composer. Buoyed by this good fortune, Verdi resigned his position in Busseto and moved with his young family to Milan to further his operatic career.

While his career was a source of increasing joy at this time, his personal life was decaying before his very eyes. He had fathered two children: a daughter, Virginia, born in March of 1837 and a son, Icilio, born in July of the following year. Within a month of his son's birth, his daughter grew gravely ill and she died one month and a day after her brother was born. No cause of death was ever found. Fourteen months later, virtually without warning, Icilio died suddenly—again, the cause was unknown. Then, only eight months later, on June 18, of 1840, Verdi lost his beloved Margherita to encephalitis. In less than two years, the young composer's family had been obliterated and his devastation knew no bounds. All during this string of tragedies, Verdi had continued to work on his second opera, *Un Giorno di Regno.* It is a comic opera, a style he would not attempt again until his final effort, *Falstaff,* premiered at the end of his life in 1893. *Un Giorno di Regno* proved a disaster on the stage and Verdi decided he would never compose again.

He canceled his contract with Merelli and became a near recluse. Several months later, quite by accident, he encountered Merelli on the street. The impresario encouraged Verdi to resume his writing and gradually, he responded. The composer referred to the next ten years of his life as "The Galley Years." He worked feverishly, producing fourteen operas over that decade—most of which were warmly received by public and critics alike. In construction, these works mainly echo the style of his famous predecessors, Donizetti and Bellini, yet Verdi's voice was unique. While he shared the gift for melody that was typical of his forbears, there was a certain rough-hewn quality about his works and his sense of the stage and his ability to present real-life feelings and characters was unsurpassed.

While most of the works of this period receive periodic performances today, several have maintained a solid place in the repertoire, particularly in Italian houses. They include *Nabucco, Ernani, Macbeth* and *Luisa Miller*. Verdi had a knack for reflecting his nation's mood and frustration over their domination by the Hapsburg Empire and many strains of his music became themes for the "risorgamento"—the national fight for independence.

Nabucco—premiered in 1842—was his first effort after the death of his wife. It is the story of the Babylonian captivity of the Jews, a subject to which the Italian populace under Austrian domination could relate well. A soaring chorus sung by the captive Hebrews, "Va, pensiero, sull'ali dorate" (Fly, thought, on golden wings), recalls the beauty of their homeland and expresses their longing for freedom. Almost from the work's first performance, this chorus became an anthem for the oppressed nation and remained so much a part of the Italian soul that at Verdi's funeral, over fifty years later, crowds lining the street spontaneously began singing it as the procession passed.

Throughout this period, Verdi became increasingly identified with the resistance. In his opera, *Attila,* for example, we hear the line "Avrai tu l'universo, resti l'Italia a me." (You may have the rest of the world, leave Italy to me.) This became the motto for the movement to unite Italy under one native ruler. In his *La Battaglia di Legnano,* there is a scene in which an imprisoned resistance officer throws himself into the river below, distraught at being kept from joining his troops in their march on the oppressor. During a performance of the work in 1849, a soldier in the audience became so caught up in the

NOEL EADIE AS GILDA, 1930

DRESS
REHEARSAL
AT THE
METROPOLITAN
OPERA,
NEW YORK

passion of the moment that he threw himself from the gallery into the orchestra pit. Incredibly, no one was hurt. Also during this time, the motto "Viva Verdi" became an ever-present phrase scrawled in graffiti on the walls of Italy's major cities. It had a double meaning: it was, first, an acknowledgment of Giuseppe Verdi as a voice for unification and it was also an acrostic for "Viva Vittorio Emmanuele, Re D'Italia" (Long live Victor Emmanuel, King of Italy). Though Verdi's personal political leanings were with those he inspired, he avoided active political involvement for most of his life, with the exception of a short period during which he served in the Italian Parliament as a representative of Busseto and its district. He was uncomfortable in this position,

however, believing himself to be ill-suited to the role of legislator.

Verdi's "Galley Years" were not solely consumed by his burgeoning career. As his spirit healed from the loss of his young family, he again found himself open to the love of a woman. Giuseppina Strepponi, a leading soprano of the time, had known and supported Verdi from his early days in Milan. She brought her influence to bear in seeing his first opera staged and she created the leading soprano role in his early triumph, *Nabucco*. Though she had abandoned the stage and made her home in Paris and he lived and worked in Italy, their

ENRICO CARUSA AS THE DUKE OF MANTUA

friendship deepened into love through frequent correspondence and periodic visits and by the latter part of the 1840's, they had taken a home together in Busseto. This was seen as an affront by his former father-in-law and mentor, Antonio Barezzi, by the composer's parents and by the self-righteous citizens of Busseto who actively shunned the couple. Barezzi wrote Verdi a scathing letter, denouncing him for his living situation and the way in which it reflected on the Barezzi family. Verdi responded calmly, affirming his admiration and gratitude for all Barezzi had done for him, but firm in his conviction that his living arrangement was a private matter. Barezzi obviously accepted Verdi's position, because the rift seemed to be mended and they continued to have personal and business dealings with one another until the elder man's death. For reasons never documented, the couple lived together for over ten years before finally marrying in 1859. Yet, Giuseppina was truly the love of his life and remained his treasured confidant and helpmate until her death in 1899, only a year and a half before Verdi's death.

In 1848, Verdi purchased a country estate at Sant'Agata. He was born to a farmer and this return to his roots was a stabilizing influence for the rest of his life. Thanks, no doubt, to his apprenticeship under the capable Signor Barezzi, he had proven himself a shrewd businessman in managing his operatic works. He turned that same business acumen toward the successful management of his sprawling farm—studying modern techniques to improve the yield of the less-than-ideal soil and hiring many local peasants whom he treated with respect and affection, thereby bolstering a shaky local economy. Over the years, it became the only environment that could fuel his artistic inspiration and his passion for carefully managing the estate contributed more to his wealth than did his musical career. He always characterized himself as a simple man from the country and it was at Sant'Agata that he was allowed to be just that.

TEATRO LA FENICE, VENICE

In the spring of 1850, Verdi was approached by the management of the Teatro La Fenice in Venice to compose a new opera for the Carnival season of 1850-51. He accepted without hesitation. Venice had produced the successful premieres of his *Ernani* and *Attila* during the previous decade and the composer held the management and artists of the house in high esteem. He had already promised an opera to his publisher for November at Trieste for which he had not yet chosen a subject. This work would be *Stiffelio,* a work that was not well received and has failed to hold the stage over the years.

He chose Francesco Maria Piave as his librettist for the new Venice project. Piave had already collaborated with Verdi on several of his most popular endeavors, including *Ernani* and *Macbeth*. Verdi suggested Victor Hugo's "Le Roi s'amuse" (The King Amuses Himself) as a subject. It was a subject that Verdi had considered for some years and his enthusiasm overrode the initial objections of his librettist and the Venetian directors. He wrote, "'Le Roi s'amuse' is one of the greatest subjects and perhaps the greatest drama of modern times. Triboulet (in the opera, Rigoletto) is a creation worthy of Shakespeare." The English bard was Verdi's favorite playwright and this was the highest compliment he could have paid the French drama. The play had been produced in 1832 in Paris and was immediately banned after the first performance. It had not been produced since, but enjoyed a wide readership due mainly to its notorious opening.

The play, in five acts, takes place in the court of Francois I of France. Though the story is not completely supported by historical fact, it paints the King as a libertine who uses his position to satisfy his lust. His jester, the hunchbacked Triboulet, serves as his accomplice in this sordid pursuit, taunting the victims of his master's conquests until he is cursed by one of the courtiers, Monsieur de Saint Vallier. Finally, the King rapes Triboulet's daughter, thinking her to be the jester's mistress. Triboulet plans revenge on the King, but his daughter's love for the degenerate monarch places her before the assassin's dagger in his place and the curse placed on Triboulet is fulfilled. It would have been difficult to choose a more provocative story for an opera. Over the previous decade, Verdi had periodic problems with the Austrian censors, who took issue with any imagined affront to their leadership, yet they had allowed many other stories of unjust rule and attempted revolution to take the stage.

Throughout the summer of 1850, Verdi believed the censors would approve the libretto. Piave had discussed the issue with some of those involved and had assured Verdi there would be no problem. It wasn't until after *Stiffelio* had its premiere in November that Verdi heard from the directors in Venice. The authorities said the production of *La Maledizione* (The Curse), the working title of *Rigoletto,* was absolutely forbidden. They expressed regret that artists of the caliber of Piave and Verdi would choose to display their talents on such "revolting immorality and obscene triviality." The communication closed with the request that no further inquiries be made in the matter. They no doubt thought the story's corrupt leader could all too easily be equated in the public mind with any number of the current Italian officials Austria had placed in power.

This edict from the censors came less than three months before the opera was scheduled to premiere and Verdi had much of the music planned in his head—if not yet on paper. He chose to fight and through a series of carefully written letters began to negotiate the future of *La Maledizione.* He proved a worthy advocate for the work and after receiving a list of proposed revisions from the authorities, he composed a long, impassioned letter which clearly defended his stand on each point of contention. After a month of wrangling, the libretto emerged relatively unscathed. In the original libretto—as in the play—the King attempts to seduce the jester's daughter after she has been abducted to the palace. She spurns him and locks herself in an adjoining room. The courtiers hand the King the key and he follows her into the room to rape her. This scene was found objectionable and deleted in the final opera. Also, the characters and the location were changed, Triboulet becoming Rigoletto, his daughter, Blanche becoming Gilda and the French King becoming the Duke of

Mantua. Beyond that, Verdi stood firm on the myriad details he had originally been asked to change. It seems odd that the censors would allow the plot to unfold in Mantua, where the possibility of comparison with a seated ruler was more immediate than if it took place in the more remote setting of sixteenth-century France. Finally, on January 25, the revised libretto was approved.

Because of the delay, the premiere was rescheduled for March 11. Some time in the middle of February, Verdi went to Venice to begin rehearsals. He conducted the rehearsals under strict privacy, not wishing to diminish the dramatic impact of his work with undue publicity. To increase the suspense, he withheld the Duke's famous aria on the fickle nature of women, "La donna è mobile," from the tenor until the day before the dress rehearsal. It is now one of the most popular arias in the tenor repertoire and legend has it that Verdi's instincts were such that he knew of its hit potential and didn't want it leaked before the premiere. Regardless of his reasons for the intrigue, the tune proved a tremendous success at the opera's opening and was soon being hummed throughout Venice.

The public recognized *Rigoletto* as a masterpiece from its first performance, but the work was not immediately well-received by the critics. *Rigoletto* marks a turning point in Verdi's development. Until this time, the characters to which he was attracted were mainly historical and one—dimensional. A character was either all good or all bad and Verdi portrayed such figures with increasing insight and skill. He now actively sought enigmatic characters; at once hostile and loving, both hero and outcast. These features are eminently apparent in *Rigoletto*. The jester is at once a loving father and an attempted assassin. Gilda, his innocent daughter is raped by a decadent ruler who first pursued her in the disguise of a student. She sacrifices her life for her rapist and he gets off scot-free. There are no unqualified heroes or completely innocent victims here and it was a challenge to the moral sensibilities of the day.

As a result, *Rigoletto* struggled for production for the first decade of its existence. Many leading censors and critics—in Italy and abroad—sought to halt its progress. Even Victor Hugo himself—no doubt jealous that his drama had been reduced to a successful libretto—managed to keep it from being performed in Paris for six years. It was finally produced in 1863 at the Paris Opera where it has played regularly ever since. In Italy, the opera played in various cities, but with the ever present cuts and adjustments of the censors, which caused Verdi's despairing remark that billboards should read "*Rigoletto, poetry and music by Don_____*" with the name of the local censor inserted.

Not all the critics objected to the controversial plot. Some took issue with the opera's construction. Verdi had contracted to produce an *opera seria* (serious opera) which had traditionally employed the aria as its basic unit of construction. *Rigoletto's* basic unit of construction is the scene and was therefore perceived as something quite new. At one point, the husband of a soprano hired to sing Gilda asked the composer to write an additional aria for the character. Verdi refused, writing: "I imagined *Rigoletto* almost without arias and without finales, just as an unbroken string of duets; because this form satisfied me." The few arias the opera does contain have all become essential repertoire for any serious singer, including the Duke's flippant "La donna è mobile," "Cortigiani, vil razza, dannata" in which Rigoletto reviles the courtiers who have abducted his daughter and the beautiful "Caro nome," in which Gilda muses about her new student suitor, Gualtier Maldé, who is actually the evil Duke in disguise.

JONATHAN MILLER'S RIGOLETTO, 1984

There were those, however, who liked Verdi's new style, finding it more versatile and more powerful dramatically. He was aware that his work was experimental and was therefore all the more pleased with its immediate success.

Prior to *Rigoletto,* Verdi had weathered the failure of a number of his operas, but after *Rigoletto* he never produced a work that did not immediately capture the public's interest and remain steadfastly in the repertoire. He had found his voice and went on to achieve some of the greatest moments the operatic stage has to offer.

With the unification of Italy and the escape from the oppressive tactics of the Austrians, *Rigoletto* was seen throughout Italy and the capitals of Europe and quickly grew in popularity. It consistently enjoys a place in the list of the top ten most frequently performed operas to this day. The role of the hunchback jester has become a mainstay of the baritone repertoire and has been portrayed by all the great baritones of the century. In 1982, the work was given renewed life by the English National Opera in an innovative production directed by Jonathan Miller and set in New York's Little Italy of the 1950's. This highly acclaimed production toured to the New York Metropolitan Opera in June of 1984. *Rigoletto* remains as chilling and spellbinding today as it was almost one hundred and fifty years ago.

The Story of the Opera

⚬

ACT I

Scene 1

The orchestra begins with a brief prelude, dominated by the theme representing the curse Monterone placed on Rigoletto.

The curtain rises on a beautiful ballroom in the ducal palace. A celebration is in progress accompanied by lively music. Throngs of courtiers and guests move about and the sounds of dancing and revelry can be heard from the inner rooms. The Duke enters in conversation with Borsa, one of the courtiers. He boasts that tonight he shall conquer the young girl he has seen repeatedly in church. Borsa inquires where she is to be found and the Duke tells him he knows where she lives and that an unknown stranger is visits her nightly. Borsa asks if she knows the identity of her suitor and the Duke responds she does not.

Borsa points out the many attractive ladies of the court. The Duke agrees they are enchanting, but none so much as the Countess Ceprano. Borsa warns him of her husband's jealousy, but the Duke responds that it would only make the conquest more appealing and goes on to voice his creed that it matters little what woman it is, her name or rank, they are all objects of his pleasure and pursuit. In spite of danger from lovers or husbands, he must conquer any woman he desires.

The guests begin a minuet and the Duke emerges from the crowd leading the Countess Ceprano by the hand. He proceeds to try to seduce her—she resists at first, but eventually she leaves the room on his arm, while her increasingly enraged husband looks on. The hunchback jester, Rigoletto, who has entered in time to see the couple's departure, derides the Count for his anger and embarrassment. The Count abruptly follows the Duke and his wife while Rigoletto involves the crowd in his malicious taunts about the Duke's latest conquest. Finally, the crippled jester limps away as the guests join in a stately court dance.

The spirited music of the scene's opening is heard again as the courtier, Marullo enters with a rich bit of gossip. He tells the assembly that it seems Rigoletto has a young lover. The courtiers are remarking that the jester seems an unlikely Cupid, when the Duke reenters—followed by Rigoletto. The Duke declares he is smitten with the Countess and asks the jester how he can get rid of the Count. Rigoletto suggests he carry her off that night and as for the Count, have him arrested or hung.

Count Ceprano has reentered and overhears this exchange. Rigoletto again begins to torment the distraught Ceprano until finally he threatens the jester with his sword. The Duke and the courtiers warn the jester to stop his taunts, but Rigoletto responds that no harm can come to him.

The whole court then turns on Rigoletto, saying they've all felt the pain of his wicked tongue and that soon revenge will be in order. The jester continues to revile them, saying that with the Duke's favor, he has nothing to fear. The tension is broken as the dancers enter from the next room calling for a return to the wine, women and song of the party.

Suddenly the voice of the Count Monterone is heard from outside, demanding he be admitted. He enters and angrily insists on speaking with the Duke. Immediately, Rigoletto begins to mimic him. Monterone announces that the Duke has dishonored his daughter and he demands retribution. His fury is only heightened by the jester's derisive comments. The Duke responds by ordering the Count's arrest, but before he can be taken from the room, he turns on the Duke, invoking a curse on him. Then, turning on Rigoletto, he says, "You who deride a father's grief, I curse you." The jester recoils in horror. The crowd then demands that the Count leave, warning him of the possible results of the Duke's indignation. He is led away by two guards as the courtiers and guests follow the Duke into an adjoining room. Rigoletto is left alone, fearfully contemplating the curse as the curtain falls.

ACT I

Scene 2

It is night in a deserted street. To the left, we see a humble dwelling with a small courtyard surrounded by a wall with a gate to the street. To the right, a large wall behind which can be seen a part of the exterior of the Ceprano palace.

The cloaked figure of Rigoletto enters and ominously repeats the curse Monterone has placed on him. A second cloaked figure enters. Sparafucile introduces himself as a man who is able to do away with an enemy or rival. He remarks that Rigoletto has a woman at his home. Fearful that the assassin may know about his daughter, Gilda, the jester changes the subject and asks his price for disposing of a nobleman. The dark figure quotes no price, saying only that half must be paid in advance. He explains that with the help of his beautiful sister he lures his victims to a tavern on the outskirts of town where they can be safely done away with. He informs Rigoletto that he can be found at this spot each night if his services are needed and, slinking away in the darkness, he repeats his name.

Alone, Rigoletto observes that he and the assassin are alike, one striking with the knife at night, the other wounding with his vicious tongue by day. He curses nature for making him the cruel and hideous caricature of a man that he is. He reflects on his handsome, carefree master and how he must always do his bidding. He raves about his hatred for the courtiers and how they use him, but his demeanor changes as he remarks that in his home, his world is different. Fearfully, he recalls Monterone's curse, then shrugging off his foreboding, enters the courtyard.

His lovely daughter runs from the house and lovingly greets him. She senses he is troubled and asks him what the secret torment is which hangs over their lives like a cloud. He avoids her question, asking if she has left the house today. She says she has gone out only to church, which puts her father's mind at ease.

She then asks him to tell her about her mother. At first he resists, but finally describes of the wonderful woman who offered him kindness and love. He breaks into sobs as he speaks of her death and Gilda attempts to comfort him.

She then asks why she is not allowed to go into the city. He responds that there are enemies there and she must never go out. He calls to Giovanna, the nurse, and implores her to keep careful watch over Gilda. The servant replies that she will.

Anxiously, Rigoletto goes out into the street to see if anyone is about. While he is out, the Duke—disguised as a student—slips into the courtyard unseen and hides behind a tree. He tosses a purse to Giovanna, buying her silence. Rigoletto reenters and asks whether anyone has followed Gilda on her return from church. Giovanna responds that no one has, and he repeats his admonition to Giovanna to protect his daughter. In an aside, the Duke expresses surprise that the beautiful young girl is the jester's daughter. Rigoletto and Gilda join their voices to express their love and bid each other farewell. He embraces his daughter and goes out again into the streets of Mantua.

Gilda sings of her guilt at not telling her father about the handsome stranger that she has seen at church. She muses about her love for him, that she doesn't care if he's rich or poor. At that moment, the Duke emerges from the shadows. Frightened, Gilda calls for Giovanna, who does not respond. Gradually, she succumbs to the Duke's declarations of love and their voices join in a passionate duet. He tells her his name is Gualtier Malde and that he is a poor, humble student.

Ceprano and Borsa are heard in the street as they identify the house as Rigoletto's—they continue on their way. Gilda hears their voices and, thinking it's her father returning, implores the Duke to leave. Giovanna enters, saying she heard footsteps and they decide to send the suitor out through the house. After a tender farewell, the Duke departs.

Alone, gazing after the Duke, Gilda repeats his name—still unaware of his true identity—as if in a trance. She rapturously savors her first feelings of love and enters the house to emerge on the balcony with a lamp to light her lover's way. She softly recalls his name again as she retreats into the house.

Meanwhile, Ceprano, Marullo, Borsa and a band of courtiers have gathered in the street below—where Rigoletto finds them as he returns home. He fails to recognize them in the darkness and they lie—telling him that they are there to abduct Ceprano's wife. Relieved to hear that their plan doesn't involve his daughter, the jester vows to join them. All are disguised, so Rigoletto consents to wearing a mask—but they equip him with one that covers his eyes. He comments on the growing darkness, as they lead him to his own home and instruct him to hold the ladder up to the wall.

They enter the house, gleefully remarking about the trick they are playing on Rigoletto and emerge with Gilda, gagged and bound. As they leave, Gilda's voice can be heard calling for help. Still holding the ladder, Rigoletto puts his hand to his face and discovers his blindfold. He tears the mask from his face and sees Gilda's scarf in the lantern's light. Insane with panic, he rushes into the house and emerges with Giovanna, whom he looks at in bewilderment. At last, he recalls Monterone's curse in horror and collapses in a faint.

ACT II

In the palace, the Duke distractedly enters the room adjoining his private chambers. He describes his return to Gilda's house, only to find her gone. He remarks that he had a feeling that she was in danger when he left and wonders who could have taken her. In a short aria, he expresses his feelings of deep and real affection for Gilda and his longing to be reunited with her.

The courtiers enter in high spirits and tell the Duke that they have abducted Rigoletto's lover and brought her to the palace. With apparently sincere joy and relief, the Duke rushes from the room, leaving the courtiers puzzled by his unexpected reaction.

From behind the scenes Rigoletto's voice is heard singing an off-handed little tune. He enters and anxiously scans the room for signs of his daughter as the courtiers greet him with mock politeness. He sees a handkerchief, which he secretly picks up as he wanders around the room, then comments that it is not Gilda's. He asks about the Duke and is told he is still asleep. They also respond suspiciously to the Duchess' page, who enters requesting an audience with the Duke. Rigoletto finally concludes that his worst fears have been realized. He asks if the girl they abducted is with the Duke in his chambers. The courtiers respond that if he has lost his lover, he must seek her elsewhere. The jester angrily tells them it is his daughter he seeks and they respond in shock. Rigoletto then launches into a diatribe against the vile courtiers who have stolen his treasure for their sport. As his rage increases, he attempts to storm the door to the Duke's chambers, but the courtiers bar his way. His energy spent and realizing they are all against him, he tearfully pleads with the noblemen to have mercy and return his daughter to him. They respond with indifference.

Suddenly, Gilda rushes into the room and throws herself into her father's arms, pouring out her feelings of shame and degradation. In a blind fury, Rigoletto turns on the courtiers, demanding that they leave him and his daughter alone. Fearful of the jester's rage, they all leave.

Alone with her father, Gilda tells of seeing the Duke at church, how he had come to their home posing as a poor student and how she loved him. In soaring phrases she recounts the abduction. Rigoletto responds in despair that it is all his fault and tries to console her as they reaffirm their love. Rigoletto then swears revenge.

Count Monterone is then led across the room to his execution. He pauses to address the Duke's portrait, saying that since his curse did not bring the Duke down—and that the Duke would no doubt live on in happiness. Rigoletto responds that the old man will be avenged. His eyes glazed in anger, the jester pours out his wrath and declares that the Duke will fall by the hand of a buffoon. Though she has been wronged, Gilda begs her father to forgive the Duke. Unwilling to hear his daughter's entreaties, the jester storms out of the palace consumed by vengeance.

ACT III

Rigoletto and Gilda approach a dilapidated inn on the banks of a river outside of Mantua. The jester questions his daughter about her feelings for the Duke. She responds that she loves him. "And even if I could prove his betrayal, would you love him still?" the father asks. Gilda responds that the Duke loves her—so Rigoletto sets out to prove his treachery. Gilda looks into the inn through a hole in the wall and sees there the murderer for hire, Sparafucile, working at the bar.

Just then, the Duke enters the inn disguised as a cavalry officer and orders wine. He demands that Sparafucile fetch his sister Maddalena. While he waits, he sings of the fickle nature of women, calling them simple and untrustworthy, but concluding that man cannot be content without them. Sparafucile reenters with a flask of wine and two glasses. After placing them on the table, he signals to his sister to come downstairs by striking sword on the ceiling. She descends in alluring gypsy dress. The Duke approaches to embrace her, but she eludes him as her brother leaves the inn to meet Rigoletto.

Perhaps the most famous ensemble in all of opera ensues as the Duke attempts to seduce the coy Maddalena inside the inn while Gilda and Rigoletto observe from outside—the jester reiterating his vengeance, his daughter pouring out her heartbroken response to what she sees and hears in the inn.

Rigoletto then turns to Gilda and tells her to go home and prepare to leave for Verona. She is to travel disguised as a man and he will join her in the morning. As she leaves, Sparafucile emerges from behind the inn and Rigoletto pays him half his required fee. He assures him the balance on completion of the job and tells the assassin he will return at midnight to retrieve the Duke's body, for he himself must throw the victim in the river. Sparafucile agrees and asks the cavalry officer's name. The jester answers that his victim's name is "Guilt," while his name is "Punishment."

Meanwhile, Maddalena is fighting off the Duke's advances inside the inn. As her brother reenters the room, she escapes the Duke's embraces and runs away. The Duke, tired of the pursuit, tells her to go to hell. She asks him to leave, but a storm is brewing and Sparafucile offers the Duke his own room for the night. He leads the Duke away as thunder rumbles in the distance and we hear the sound of a rising wind. The Duke has cast his spell on Maddalena— when Sparafucile returns, she pleads with her brother to spare his life. While they argue his fate, Gilda returns, dressed in men's clothing, compelled to ignore her father's instructions because of her love for the Duke.

Maddalena insists she cannot allow the Duke to die, but her brother only tosses her the bag in which he will deliver the corpse, ordering her to mend it. She suggests he kill Rigoletto instead when he comes to pay the balance of the fee. Gilda listens in horror. Sparafucile refuses, but finally agrees to kill the first person who comes to the door before Rigoletto's return and spare the Duke. As the storm intensifies, their voices join in an impassioned trio with Gilda praying for strength, Maddalena exulting at having saved her lover and Sparafucile repeating the terms of the deal. As the storm approaches its height, the clock strikes 11:30 and Gilda, determined to save the Duke, knocks at the inn door. When the assassin answers the door, she claims to be a stranger, lost in the storm. As she enters, Sparafucile attacks and stabs her with his dagger. The storm rises to a terrible fury, then begins to subside.

As the storm dies away, Rigoletto returns, happy to have revenge at last. The clock strikes midnight and he knocks on the inn door. Sparafucile answers and delivers the grim sack containing Gilda's body. Rigoletto pays him, then turns to take the corpse to the river when he hears the Duke singing his flippant tune about the unpredictability of women.

Rigoletto is frozen by the sound of the Duke's voice and as its sound fades, he opens the sack, only to find his dying daughter. Frantic, he knocks at the door of the inn—there is no answer. In desperation, he calls his daughter's name. Gilda stirs, then recognizes her father. He demands to know how it happened; who did this to her. She confesses she alone is responsible for her fate. She has given her life for her love. Rigoletto is overcome with remorse that his beloved daughter has become the innocent victim of his own need for vengeance. Failing, she tells her father she will soon join her mother; she asks for his blessing and forgiveness of the Duke. She promises him her prayers, then falls dead in his arms.

He tentatively calls her name, then in a sudden horrible realization, recalls the curse of Monterone and collapses in despair over his daughter's body as the curtain falls.

The Artists

Beverly Sills (**Gilda**) For over fifty years, Beverly Sills has championed opera in every facet of her life: as singer, administrator and American artist par excellence. Born Belle Silvermann in Brooklyn, New York, she began her public career at the ripe age of three, singing on the radio. She "retired" at the twelve to pursue her studies—which included Italian, French, piano and vocal study with the esteemed Estelle Liebling. At sixteen, she toured with the Schubert Opera Company in operetta roles and the following year debuted with both the Philadelphia Civic Opera and the San Francisco Opera Company.

In 1955 she joined the roster of the New York City Opera, receiving wide attention for her portrayal of Baby Doe Tabor in the New York premiere of Douglas Moore's *The Ballad of Baby Doe*. In 1965, she portrayed all three heroines in Offenbach's *The Tales of Hoffman* and in 1966 her portrayal of Cleopatra in Handel's *Julius Ceasar* launched her international career.

She soon conquered all the great European houses, specializing in the Italian bel canto roles of Rossini and Donizetti—achieving particular success in

BEVERLY SILLS AND HER DAUGHTER MUFFY, 1970

her portrayals of all three of Donizetti's Tudor queens, Maria Stuarda, Anna Bolena and Elizabeth I in *Roberto Devereaux*. In 1975 she made her long-awaited Metropolitan Opera debut as Pamira in Rossini's *The Siege of Corinth*.

Her repertoire includes over fifty roles—from the Baroque rarity of Rameau's *Hippolyte et Aricie* to the twelve-tone intricacies of Nono's *Intolleranza* and including everything in between. She did a great deal to enhance the country's exposure to and understanding of opera by her frequent appearances on popular TV talk shows and in television specials—the most memorable of which paired her with the famous musical theatre artist, Julie Andrews.

After her retirement from the operatic stage, she took over the reins as General Director of the New York City Opera, which she ran with distinction from 1979 to 1989. Today, she presides over the Board of Directors of Lincoln Center in New York, home of New York City Opera and the MET, both houses she graced with her marvelous performing talents.

Always possessed of an incredible sweetness of sound, her portrayal of Gilda is exquisite—portraying the gentle youth of the poor lovesick ingenue with perfect understanding and taste. This is a truly great performance by a truly great lady of the operatic stage.

Sherrill Milnes (Rigoletto) Sherrill Milnes is one of the greatest baritones of the twentieth century. He was born in 1935 in Downers Grove, Illinois. He studied at Drake University and Northwestern and with the famous soprano, Rosa Ponselle. He honed his craft touring with the Boris Goldovsky opera company, a famous training ground for many young American artists. In 1962, he won a Ford Foundation Award, which sponsored appearances with the opera companies of Houston, Pittsburgh, San Antonio, Central City and Cincinnati and in 1964, he won the American Opera Auditions. That same year he joined the roster of the New York City Opera and his success there led to his Metropolitan Opera debut in December of 1965 as Valentin in Gounod's *Faust*.

He remained a leading baritone at the MET for over twenty-five years. Specializing in the Verdi baritone roles, he inherited the standard from a long

SHERILL MILNES AND KIRI TE KANAWA IN VERDI'S SIMON BOCCANEGRA, 1980

line of famous American Verdi interpreters, including Lawrence Tibbett, Leonard Warren and Robert Merrill. Yet, his repertoire is large and eclectic. In 1967, he created the role of Adam Brant in Marvin David Levy's *Mourning Becomes Electra* and the American Premiere of *The Fiery Angel* is included in his credits. Renowned for his acting abilities, he has sung most of the great baritone roles of the repertoire, including Figaro in *The Barber of Seville,* Escamillo in *Carmen,* Tonio in *I Pagliacci,* Gerard in *Andrea Chenier* and a host of others from the French and Italian repertoire. In recent years, he has added a number of Wagnerian roles to his credits.

Throughout the 1970s, Milnes went on to conquer the stages of all the major opera houses of the world. He began at the Vienna Staatsoper in 1970 and moved on to the Teatro Colon in Buenos Aires, the Hamburg and Paris Operas, the Munich Opera in 1976 and concluded with a triumphant La Scala debut in 1978.

He has sung all the major Verdi baritone roles and has recorded the role of Rigoletto twice. In 1991 he added the mature role of Falstaff to his Verdi portrayals to wide acclaim. He divides his time today between performing and teaching, having distinguished himself as a brilliant adjudicator in master classes throughout the country. Possessing a voice of incredible beauty, with a broad range of colors and dynamic nuance, coupled with ringing and easy high notes, Milnes in the quintessential Verdi baritone and his portrayal of the hunchback jester heard here is perfect testimony to his greatness.

Alfredo Kraus (The Duke of Mantua) Kraus was born of German and Spanish parentage in the Canary Islands. As a young man, he completed his studies in engineering at his father's request before embarking on the pursuit of his first love, singing. After studies with Mercedes Llopart, he made his professional debut in 1956 at the Cairo Opera in the role heard here, the Duke in *Rigoletto.* His success grew as he appeared in various Italian theaters and in Spain. He made his Covent Garden debut in 1959 and the following year, he sang the role of Edgardo in Donizetti's *Lucia di Lamermoor* opposite the famous Australian soprano, Joan Sutherland at La Scala. Triumphs in the world's most estimable houses followed in short order. He maintained a long-standing place on the stage of New York's Metropolitan Opera, performing there regularly well into his sixties.

Kraus is a light lyric tenor, specializing in the roles of Donizetti, Rossini, Mozart and Massanet's Des Grieux in *Manon* and the title role in *Werther*. Possessed of a beautiful, flexible voice, he is renowned as an extremely intelligent artist, considered the best in his field throughout his long career and having an exceptional high range extending to high "d". Because he so carefully preserved his delicate instrument, he remains at his best even in performances today.

Like Sherrill Milnes, he has recorded the Duke more than once and though he finds the character unsympathetic, the role has figured prominently in his career. Besides portraying the Duke for his Cairo debut, it was also the vehicle for his MET debut in the old house in 1966. His unequaled sense of style and elegance, combined with a warmth of expression and handsome stage presence have rendered him one of the greatest tenors of his generation—the best of his art is demonstrated on this recording.

Samuel Ramey (Sparafucile) Born and raised in the tiny western Kansas town of Colby, Sam Ramey has become an opera rarity—a Basso star. He studied at Wichita State University in Kansas with Arthur Newman, a former member of the New York City Opera roster and established himself at City Opera with a 1973 debut as Zuniga in *Carmen*. Upon the death of their leading bass, Norman Treigle, Sam began to take on many of the roles he had made famous, including Olin Blitch in Carlisle Floyd's Susannah and the title role in Arrigo Boito's *Mephistophele*.

His success at New York's state theatre soon led to engagements all over the world. It would be difficult to name a major house where he has not triumphed. Boasting a huge and diverse repertoire from the works of Handel to Stravinsky, he is one of the most recorded basses in history.

Sam is particularly famous for his exhaustive portrayals of the devil, including roles in Mozart's *Don Giovanni,* Berlioz' *Damnation of Faust,* Stravinsky's *The Rake's Progress* and both Gounod's and Boito's Mephistopheles. He is an active recitalist and has recorded many American songs, a superb actor, with "matinee idol" looks that have made him one of the world's most sought-after singers. His resonant, flexible voice is the ideal addition to this exquisite cast.

Mignon Dunn (Maddalena) Mignon Dunn was born in Memphis Tennessee in 1931. Like Sills, Milnes and Ramey, she is an American success story. She studied in New York with Karin Branzell and made her debut as Carmen in New Orleans. She debuted at City Opera in New York in 1956 and at the Metropolitan in 1958. She has been a mainstay of the company ever since and her breadth is impressive—her repertoire includes French, Italian and German roles.

She has had successful engagements with most of the country's leading opera houses, including San Francisco and Chicago. Known for the rich, dramatic quality of her voice, she has distinguished herself in all the major roles of the mezzo-soprano repertoire.

Julius Rudel (Conductor) Maestro Rudel has had a profound effect on the world of opera in the United States over a distinguished career which spanned fifty-five years. Born in Vienna in 1921, he came to the United States at seventeen. Having begun his musical studies at the Vienna Academy, he continued at the Mannes School of Music in New York.

He joined the music staff of the New York City Opera in 1943, making his conducting debut the following year with *The Gypsy Baron*. From 1957 to 1979, he held the post of artistic director for the City Opera, elevating the company to a position of great respect among American opera houses. Under his leadership, the New York State Theatre became known for its ensemble approach to casting, its creative productions and its willingness to stage new works including Argento's *Miss Havisham's Fire,* Ellstein's *The Golem* and Carlisle Floyd's *Jonathan Wade.* He was also instrumental in advancing Alberto Ginastera's career, conducting the premieres of three of his operas: *Bomarzo, Don Rodrigo* and *Beatrix Cenci.*

Not only a conductor, he became adept at every facet of opera management and production and is highly regarded by his colleagues. He was instrumental in launching the careers of many important singers, including Beverly Sills and Samuel Ramey, both heard on this recording.

In 1978, he made his Metropolitan Opera debut, conducting Massanet's *Werther* and has been a frequent guest there ever since. Rudel also appears frequently in Europe, conducting at the Paris Opera, the Vienna Staatsoper and Covent Garden, among others.

His repertoire includes over 140 works ranging from Monteverdi to Kurt Weill and every conceivable style in between. Today he continues to maintain an active schedule, bringing the benefit of his award-winning experience to opera audiences the world over.

The Libretto

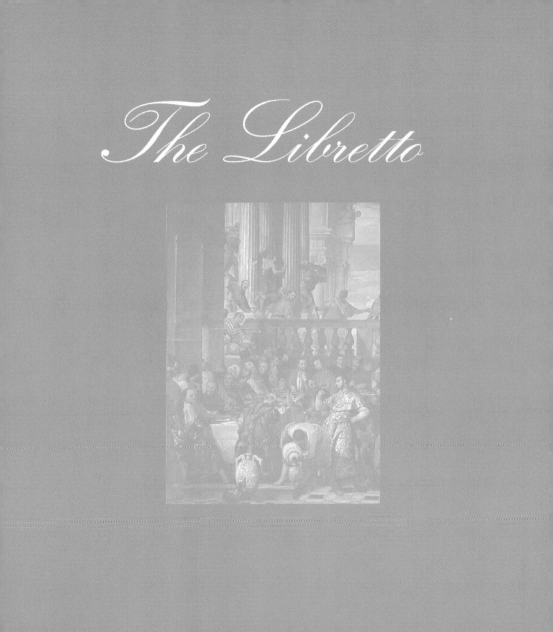

Act 1

CD 1/Track 1 *Prelude* The theme associated with Rigoletto's fearful recollection of Monterone's curse dominates the short orchestral prelude. This ominous theme builds to a climax (01:15) built from a theme sung in several guises by Gilda throughout the opera and heard here in a full-throated, desperate minor key, then subsides to a quiet restatement of the "curse" theme.

Scene 1

PRELUDE

A magnificent hall in the Ducal Palace, Mantua

(Doors at the far end lead to other rooms; all are splendidly illuminated and thronged with a courtly company of knights and ladies in rich attire. Pages pass to and fro. The merrymaking is at its height. From within, the sound of music. The Duke and Borsa emerge from a door at the far end.)

CD 1/Track 2 The mood changes abruptly as the curtain opens on a lively party in the Duke's palace.

DUCA
Della mia bella incognita borghese
toccare il fin dell'avventura voglio.

DUKE
I intend to clinch my affair
with that nameless beauty of the
bourgeoisie.

BORSA
Di quella giovin che vedete al tempio?

BORSA
The girl you've seen in church?

DUCA
Da tre mesi ogni festa.

DUKE
Every feastday for the past three months.

BORSA
La sua dimora?

BORSA
Where does she live?

DUCA
In un remoto calle;
misterioso un uom v'entra ogni notte.

DUKE
In a quiet backalley;
a mysterious man goes there every night.

BORSA
E sa colei chi sia l'amante suo?

BORSA
And does she know who her admirer is?

DUCA
Lo ignora.

DUKE
No, she doesn't.

A group of ladies with their cavaliers cross the room.

BORSA
Quante beltà! Mirate.

BORSA
What a bunch of beauties! Look at them!

DUCA
Le vince tutte di Cepran la sposa.

DUKE
But Ceprano's wife beats them all.

BORSA
Non v'oda il Conte, o Duca!

BORSA
Don't let the Count hear you, my lord!

DUCA
A me che importa?

DUKE
What do I care?

BORSA
Dirlo ad altra ei potria.

BORSA
He might tell another woman.

CD 1/Track 3   *"Questo e quella"* The frivolous charm of this short, well-known aria con-
trasts with the lascivious philosophy the Duke is expressing.

DUCA
Né sventura per me certo saria.
Questa o quella per me pari sono
a quant'altre d'intorno mi vedo;
dei mio core l'impero non cedo
meglio ad una che ad altra beltà.
La costoro avvenenza è qual dono
di che il fato ne infiora la vita;
s'oggi questa mi torna gradita
forse un'altra doman lo sarà.
La costanza, tiranna dei core,
detestiamo qual morbo crudele.
Sol chi vuole si serbi fedele;
non v'è amor se non v'è libertà,
De' mariti il geloso furore,
degli amanti le smanie derido;
anco d'Argo i cent'occhi disfido
se mi punge una qualche beltà.

DUKE
That wouldn't worry me at all.
Neither is any different
from the rest I see around me;
I never yield my heart
to one beauty more than another.
Feminine charm is a gift bestowed
by fate to brighten our lives.
And if one woman pleases me today,
tomorrow, like as not, another will.
Fidelity that tyrant of the heart
we shun like pestilence.
Only those who want to should be faithful;
without freedom there is no love.
I find the ravings of jealous husbands
and the frenzy of lovers ridiculous;
once smitten by a pretty face
I'd not let Argus' hundred eyes deter me!

*Count Ceprano enters and, from a distance, watches his wife who is
on the arm of another man; more ladies and gentlemen enter.*

DUCA *(alla signora di Ceprano movendo ad
incontrarla con molta galanteria)*
  Partite? Crudele!

DUKE *(to Ceprano's wife, greeting her with
great gallantry)*
You are leaving us? How cruel!

CONTESSA DI CEPRANO
Seguire lo sposo m'è forza a Ceprano.

COUNTESS CEPRANO
I must go with my husband to Ceprano

DUCA
Ma dee luminoso
in corte tal astro qual sole brillare.

Per voi qui ciascuno dovrà palpitare.

Per voi già possente la fiamma d'amore
inebria, conquide, distrugge il mio coro.

DUKE
So bright a star
should be shedding its brilliance on my
court.
You would make every heart beat faster
here.
The fires of passion already flare
headily, conquering, consuming my heart.

He kisses her hand fervently.

CONTESSA
Calmatevi!

COUNTESS
Calm yourself!
The fires of passion already flare, etc.

DUCA
La fiamma d'amore inebria, ecc.

CONTESSA
Calmatevi!

COUNTESS
Calm yourself!

The Duke gives her his arm and leads her out.

RIGOLETTO *(entrando che s'incontra nel signor di Coprano)*
In testa che avete,
Signor di Coprano?

RIGOLETTO *(entering, meeting Count Ceprano)*
What have you on your head,
my lord of Ceprano?

Ceprano reacts with an angry gesture, then follows his wife and the Duke.
to the Courtiers

Ei sbuffa, vedete?

He's fuming, did you see?

BORSA, CORTIGIANI
Che festa!

BORSA, COURTIERS
What sport!

RIGOLETTO
Oh s'i…

RIGOLETTO
Oh, yes!

BORSA, CORTIGIANI
Il Duca qui pur si diverte!

BORSA, COURTIERS
The Duke is enjoying himself!

RIGOLETTO
Così non è sempre? che nuove scoperte!
li giuoco ed il vino, le feste, la danza,
battaglie, conviti, ben tutto gli sta.

RIGOLETTO
Doesn't he always? That's nothing new.
Gaming and wine, parties, dancing,
battles and banquets anything goes.

Or della Contessa l'assedio egli avanza,
e intanto il marito fremendo ne va.

He leaves the room.

MARULLO *(entrando premuroso)*
Gran nuova! Gran nuova!

CORTIGIANI
Che avvenne? parlate!

MARULLO
Stupir ne dovrete!

CORTIGIANI, BORSA
Narrate, narrate.

MARULLO
Ah! ah! Rigoletto…

CORTIGIANI, BORSA
Ebben?

MARULLO
Caso enorme!

CORTIGIANI, BORSA
Perduto ha la gobba? non è più
difforine?

MARULLO
Più strana è la cosa! Il pazzo possiede…

CORTIGIANI, BORSA
Infine?

Now he's laying siege to the Countess
while her husband goes off in a rage.

MARULLO *(entering excitedly)*
Great news! Great news!

COURTIERS
What has happened? Tell us!

MARULLO
This will amaze you!

COURTIERS. BORSA
Tell us, tell us.

MARULLO
Ah Ah! Rigoletto…

COURTIERS, BORSA
Well?

MARULLO
Against all the odds…

COURTIERS, BORSA
He's lost his hump? He's no longer a
monster?

MARULLO
Even more extraordinary! The fool has…

COURTIERS, BORSA
Has what?

MARULLO
Un'amante.

CORTIGIANI, BORSA
Un'amante! Chi il crede?

MARULLO
Il gobbo in Cupido or s'è trasformato.

CORTIGIANI, BORSA
Quel mostro? Cupido!

TUTTI
Cupido beato!

The Duke returns followed by Rigoletto then Ceprano.

DUCA *(a Rigoletto)*
Ah, più di Ceprano importuno non v'è!
La cara sua sposa è un angiol per me!

RIGOLETTO
Rapitela.

DUCA
L detto; ma il farlo?

RIGOLETTO
Stasera.

DUCA
Non pensi tu al Conte?

RIGOLETTO
Non c'è la prigione?

MARULLO
A mistress!

COURTIERS, BORSA
A mistress! Who'd ever believe it?

MARULLO
The hunchback has changed into Cupid.

COURTIERS, BORSA
That monster? Cupid?

ALL
Some Cupid!

DUKE *(to Rigoletto)*
An, no one is such a bore as Ceprano!
And his dear wife is an angel!

RIGOLETTO
Carry her off.

DUKE
Easy to say; but how?

RIGOLETTO
Tonight.

DUKE
Have you forgotten the Count?

RIGOLETTO
What about prison?

DUCA
Ah, no.

RIGOLETTO
Ebben, s'esilia.

DUCA
Nemmeno, buffone.

RIGOLETTO (*indicando di farla tagliare*)
Allora la testa…

CEPRANO (**FRA SÉ**)
Quell'anima nera!

DUCA (*battendo colla mano una spalla al Conte*)
Che di', questa testa?

RIGOLETTO
L ben naturale.
Che fare di tal testa?
A cosa ella vale?

CEPRANO (*infuriato, brandendo la spada*)
Marrano!

DUCA (*a Ceprano*)
Fermate!

RIGOLETTO
Da rider mi fa.

MARULLO, CORTIGIANI (*tra loro*)
In furia è montato!

DUCA (*a Rigoletto*)
Buffone, vien qua.

DUKE
Ah, no.

RIGOLETTO
Well, banish him, then.

DUKE
Not that either, fool.

RIGOLETTO (*with a graphic gesture*)
Well then, his head…

CEPRANO (*to himself*)
The blackhearted villain!

DUKE (*clapping the Count on the shoulder*)
What, this head?

RIGOLETTO
Naturally.
What else can you do with such a head?
What's it good for?

CEPRANO (*furiously, drawing his sword*)
Scoundrel!

DUKE (**TO CEPRANO**)
That's enough!

RIGOLETTO
He makes me laugh.

MARULLO, COURTIERS (*to each other*)
He's furious!

DUKE (*to Rigoletto*)
Fool, come here.

BORSA, MARULLO, CORTIGIANI
In furia è montato!

DUCA
Ah, sempre tu spingi lo scherzo
all'estremo.
Quell'ira che sfidi colpirti potrà.

CEPRANO *(ai Cortigiani a parte)*
Vendetta dei pazzo!

RIGOLETTO
Che coglier mi puote? Di loro non temo;
del Duca un protetto nessun toccherà.

CEPRANO
Contr'esso un rancore
di noi chi non ha?
Vendetta!

BORSA, MARULLO, CORTIGIANI *(a Ceprano)*
Ma come?

CEPRANO
In armi chi ha core
doman sia da me.

BORSA, MARULLO, CORTIGIANI
Sì.

CEPRANO
A notte.

BORSA, MARULLO, CORTIGIANI
Sarà.

BORSA, MARULLO, COURTIERS
He's in a fury!

DUKE
You always take a joke too far.
The wrath you provoke could rebound
upon you.

CEPRANO *(to the courtiers)*
Revenge on the fool!

RIGOLETTO
Who could harm me? I'm not afraid of them.
No one dare touch a favourite of the Duke.

CEPRANO
Which of us nurses
no grudge against him?
Revenge!

BORSA, MARULLO, COURTIERS *(to Ceprano)*
But how?

CEPRANO
Let those with spirit come armed
to my house tomorrow.

BORSA, MARULLO, COURTIERS
Yes!

CEPRANO
After dark.

BORSA, MARULLO, COURTIERS
Agreed.

RIGOLETTO
Che Coglier mi puote? *ecc.*

DUCA
Ah, sempre tu spingi lo scherzo, ecc.

BORSA, CEPRANO, MARULLO, CORTIGIANI
Vendetta dei pazzo!
Contr'esso un rancore
pei tristi suoi modi
di noi chi non ha?
Si, vendetta! ecc.
Sì, vendetta!

DUCA, RIGOLETTO
Tutto è gioia, tutto è festa!
(La folla de' danzatori invade la scena.)

TUTTI
Tutto è gioia, tutto è festa!
Tutto invitaci a goder!
Oh, guardate, non par questa
or la reggia dei piacer?

Enter Count Monterone.

RIGOLETTO
Who could harm me? *etc.*

DUCA
Ah, you always take a joke, etc.

BORSA, CEPRANO, MARULLO, CORTIGIANI
Revenge on the fool!
Which of us nurses
no grudge against him
for his cruel ways?
Yes, revenge! etc.
Yes, revenge!

DUKE, RIGOLETTO
What gaiety! What a party spirit!
(The dancers swirl into the room.)

ALL
What gaiety! What party spirit!
What splendid entertainment!
Oh, just look, would you not say
that this was the realm of pleasure?

CD 1/Track 7   The party mood is interrupted by the entrance of Monterone, whose daughter
has been seduced by the Duke.

MONTERONE *(da lontano)*
Ch'io gli parli.

DUCA
No.

MONTERONE
Let me speak to him.

DUKE
No!

MONTERONE *(avanzando)*
Il voglio.

BORSA, RIGOLETTO, MARULLO, CEPRANO,
CORTIGIANI
Monterone!

MONTERONE *(fissando il Duca, con nobile
orgoglio)*
Sì, Monteron. La voce mia qual tuono
vi scuoterà dovunque…

RIGOLETTO *(al Duca, contraffacendo la voce di
Monterone)*
Ch'io gli parli.

advancing with mocksolemnity

Voi congiuraste contro noi, signore,
e noi, clementi invero, perdonammo.
Qual vi piglia or delirio a tutte l'ore
di vostra figlia a reclamar l'onore?

MONTERONE *(guardando Rigoletto con ira
sprezzante)*
Novello insulto!
(al Duca)
Ah s'i, a turbare
sarò vostr'orgie; verrò a gridare
fino a che vegga restarsi inulto
di mia famiglia l'atroce insulto;
e se al carnefice pur mi darete,
spettro terribile mi rivedrete,
portante in mano il teschio mio.
vendetta chiedere al mondo e a Dio.

MONTERONE **(COMING FORWARD)**
I shall!

BORSA, RIGOLETTO, MARULLO, CEPRANO,
CORTIGIANI
Monterone!

MONTERONE *(fixing the Duke with a took of
fearless pride)*
Yes, Monterone. My voice, like thunder,
shall make you quake wherever you go

RIGOLETTO *(to the Duke, imitating
Monterone)*
Let me speak to him.

You did conspire against us, my lord,
and we, with royal clemency, forgave you.
What mad impulse is this, that night and day
you make complaint about your daughter's
honour?

MONTERONE *(regarding Rigoletto with angry
contempt)*
One more insult!
(to the Duke)
Ah yes! I shall disrupt
your orgies; I shall come here to complain
so long as the atrocious insult
to my family remains unpunished.
And if you give me over to your hangman,
I shall haunt you as a terrifying spectre,
carrying my skull in my hands,
crying to God and man for vengeance!

DUCA
Non più, arrestatelo.

RIGOLETTO
L matto.

CORTIGIANI
Quai detti!

MONTERONE *(al Duca e Rigoletto)*
Oh, siate entrambi voi maledetti!

BORSA, MARULLO, CEPRANO, CORTIGIANI
Ah!

MONTERONE
Sianciare il cane a leon morente
è vile, o Duca
(meno Rigoletto)
E tu, serpente,
tu che d'un padre ridi al dolore,
si maledetto!

RIGOLETTO *(da sé, colpito)*
Che sento! orrore!

TUTTI *(meno Rigoletto) (a Monterone)*
O tu che la festa audace hai turbato
da un genio d'inferno qui fosti guidato;
è vano ogni detto, di qua t'allontana,
va, trema, o vegliardo, dell'ira sovrana,
ecc.

DUKE
Enough! Arrest him.

RIGOLETTO
He's mad.

CORTIGIANI
What audacity!

MONTERONE *(to the Duke and Rigoletto)*
May both of you be damned!

BORSA, MARULLO, CEPRANO, COURTIERS
Ah!

MONTERONE
To unleash your hounds on a dying lion
is cowardly, o Duke.
(to Rigoletto)
and you, you serpent,
you who ridicule a father's grief,
my curse upon you!

RIGOLETTO *(aside, horrorstruck)*
What has he said! Alas!

ALL *(except Rigoletto) (to Monterone)*
O you who so daringly disrupt our revels,
some demon from hell must have guided
you here;
no words will avail you, begone from
this place,
go, greybeard, beware of your sovereign's
wrath.

RIGOLETTO
Orrore!
Che orrore! *ecc.*

RIGOLETTO
Horror!
What horror! *etc.*

MONTERONE
Sii maledetto! E tu serpente! ecc.

MONTERONE
My curse upon you! And you, you
serpent! etc.

TUTTI *(meno Rigoletto)*
Tu l'hai provocata, più speme von v'è,
un'ora fatale fu questa per te.
(Monterone parte fra due alabardieri;
tutti gli altri seguono il Duca in altra
stanza.)

ALL *(except Rigoletto)*
You have provoked it, all hope is lost,
this was a fatal mistake on your part.
(Monterone goes out between two
halberdiers. The others all follow the
Duke into an adjoining room.)

Scena 2

*The end of a culdesac (Left, a modest house with a small courtyard enclosed by
walls. In the courtyard, a large tree with a marble bench beside it; a door in the
wall opens on to the street. Above the wall, a terrace over a loggia. From the second
storey a door opens on to the terrace, which is reached by a flight of steps in front. To
the right of the road, a much higher wall surrounding the garden and one side of
the Ceprano palace. It is night. Rigoletto enters, wrapped in a cloak. Sparafucile, a
long sword beneath his cloak, follows him.)*

CD 1/Track 9   The second scene begins with the same musical motive we heard at the beginning of the prelude. Rigoletto is obsessed by the curse Monterone has placed
on him.

RIGOLETTO *(da sé)*
Quel vecchio maledivami!

RIGOLETTO *(to himself)*
The old man cursed me!

SPARAFUCILE
Signor?…

SPARAFUCILE
Signor?…

RIGOLETTO
Va, non ho niente.

RIGOLETTO
Go I have nothing.

SPARAFUCILE
Né il chiesi: a voi presente
un uom di spada sta.

RIGOLETTO
Un ladro?

SPARAFUCILE
Un uom che libera
per poco da un rivale,
e voi ne avete.

RIGOLETTO
Quale?

SPARAFUCILE
La vostra donna è là.

RIGOLETTO *(da sé)*
Che sento!
(a Sparafucile)
E quanto spendere
per un signore dovrei?

SPARAFUCILE
Prezzo maggior vorrei.

RIGOLETTO
Com'usasi pagar?

SPARAFUCILE
Una metà s'anticipa, il resto si dà poi.

RIGOLETTO *(da sé)*
Demonio!
(a Sparafucile)

SPARAFUCILE
And I asked for nothing. You see before
you a swordsman.

RIGOLETTO
A robber?

SPARAFUCILE
One who can rid you,
for a small fee, of a rival,
which you have.

RIGOLETTO
Who?

SPARAFUCILE
Your woman lives there.

RIGOLETTO *(to himself)*
What's this!
(to Sparafucile)
And how much
would you charge me for a nobleman?

SPARAFUCILE
I'd demand a higher price.

RIGOLETTO
How are you usually paid?

SPARAFUCILE
Half in advance, the rest on completion.

RIGOLETTO *(to himself)*
The demon!
(to Sparafucile)

E come puoi
tanto securo oprar?

SPARAFUCILE
Soglio in cittade uccidere,
oppure nel mio tetto.
L'uomo di sera aspetto;
una stoccata e muor.

RIGOLETTO (da sé)
Demonio!
(a Sparafucile)
E come in casa?

SPARAFUCILE
E facile.
M'aiuta mia sorella.
Per le vie danza…è bella…
Chi voglio attira, e allor…

RIGOLETTO
Comprendo.

SPARAFUCILE
Senza strepito…

RIGOLETTO
Comprendo.

SPARAFUCILE
E questo il mio strumento.

indicating his sword

Vi serve?

And how is it
that you can work so safely?

SPARAFUCILE
I either kill in the town
or under my own roof.
I wait for my man at night;
one thrust and he dies.

RIGOLETTO (to himself)
The demon!
(to Sparafucile)
And how do you work at home?

SPARAFUCILE
It's simple.
My sister helps me.
She dances in the streets…she's pretty…
she entices the victim, and then…

RIGOLETTO
I understand.

SPARAFUCILE
Without a sound…

RIGOLETTO
I understand.

SPARAFUCILE
This is my instrument.

Can it serve you?

RIGOLETTO
No…al momento.

SPARAFUCILE
Peggio per voi.

RIGOLETTO
Chisa?

SPARAFUCILE
Sparafucil mi nomino.

RIGOLETTO
Straniero?

SPARAFUCILE *(per andarsene)*
Borgognone.

RIGOLETTO
E dove all'occasione?

SPARAFUCILE
Qui sempre a sera.

RIGOLETTO
Va.

SPARAFUCILE
Sparafucil, Sparafucil.

RIGOLETTO
No…not just now.

SPARAFUCILE
You'll regret it.

RIGOLETTO
Who knows?

SPARAFUCILE
My name is Sparafucile

RIGOLETTO
A foreigner?

SPARAFUCILE *(as he leaves)*
Burgundian.

RIGOLETTO
And where, if the need should arise?

SPARAFUCILE
Here, each night.

RIGOLETTO
Go!

SPARAFUCILE
Sparafucile, Sparafucile.

He leaves.

CD 1/Track 10   In the powerful monologue, "Pari siamo!" we encounter Rigoletto in all his tortured humanity. He rages against his deformity and the courtiers who use him for their sport, but in his home, his life transcends the dark folly of the court.

RIGOLETTO
(guarda dietro a Sparafucile)
Va,va,va,va.
Pari siamo!…io la lingua,
egli ha il pugnale.
L'uomo son io che ride,
ei quel che spegne!
Quei vecchio maledivarni…
O uomini! o natura!
Vil scellerato mi faceste voi!
O rabbia! esser difforme, esser buffone!
Non dover, non poter altro che ridere!
Il retaggio d'ogni uom m'è tolto, il pianto.
Questo padrone mio,
giovin, giocondo, s'i possente, bello,
sonnecchiando mi dice:
Fa ch'io rida, buffone!
Forzarmi deggio e farlo! Oh dannazione!
Odio a voi, cortigiani schernitori!
Quanta in mordervi ho gioia!
Se iniquo son, per cagion vostra è solo.
Ma in altr'uomo qui mi cangio!…
Quel vecchio maledivami!…Tal pensiero
perché conturba ognor la mente mia?
Mi coglierà sventura?
Ah no, è follia!

RIGOLETTO
(his gaze following Sparafucile)
Go, go, go, go.
We are two of a kind: my weapon is my tongue,
his is a dagger;
I am a man of laughter,
he strikes the fatal blow!
The old man cursed me
O mankind! O nature!
It was you who made me evil and corrupt!
I rage at my monstrous form, my cap and bells!
To be permitted nothing but to laugh!
I'm denied that common human right, to weep.
My master,
young, carefree, so powerful, so handsome,
halfdozing, says:
"Fool, make me laugh!"
And I must contrive to do it! Oh, damnation!
My hate upon you, sneering courtiers!
How I enjoy snapping at your heels!
If I am wicked, the fault is yours alone.
But here I become another person!
The old man cursed me! Why should this thought still prey so on my mind?
Will some disaster befall me?
Ah no, this is folly!

He opens the gate with a key and enters the courtyard. Gilda runs from the house and into his arms.

Figlia!

My daughter!

GILDA
Mio padre!

GILDA
Father!

RIGOLETTO
A te d'appresso
trova sol gioia il core oppresso.

GILDA
Oh, quanto amore, padre mio!

RIGOLETTO
Mia vita sei!

GILDA
Oh, quanto amore!

RIGOLETTO
Senza te in terra qual bene avrei?

GILDA
Oh, quant'amore, padre mio!

RIGOLETTO
Ah, figlia mia!

GILDA
Voi sospirate! che v'ange tanto?
Lo dite a questa povera figiia.
Se v'ha mistero, per lei sia franto:
ch'ella conosca la sua famiglia.

RIGOLETTO
Tu non ne hai.

GILDA
Qual nome avete?

RIGOLETTO
A te che importa?

RIGOLETTO
Only with you
does my heavy heart find joy.

GILDA
Oh, how loving you are. father!

RIGOLETTO
You are my life!

GILDA
Oh, how loving you are!

RIGOLETTO
Without you, what would I have on earth?

GILDA
How loving you are, father!

RIGOLETTO
Ah my daughter!

GILDA
You sigh! What makes you so sad?
Tell your poor daughter.
If you have secrets, share them with her:
let her know about her family.

RIGOLETTO
You have no family.

GILDA
What is your name?

RIGOLETTO
What does it matter?

GILDA
Se non volete
di voi parlarmi…

RIGOLETTO *(interrompendola)*
Non uscir mai.

GILDA
Non vo che al tempio.

RIGOLETTO
Oh, ben tu fai.

GILDA
Se non di voi, almen chi sia
fate ch'io sappia la madre mia.

RIGOLETTO
Deh, non parlare al misero
dei suo perduto bene.
Ella sentia, quell'angelo,
pietà delle mie pene.
Solo, difforme, povero,
per compassion mi amò.
Morla…le zolle coprano
lievi quel capo amato.
Sola or tu resti al misero…
O Dio, sii ringraziato!

GILDA *(singhiozzando)*
Oh quanto dolor! che spremere
sì amaro pianto può?
Padre, non più, calmatevi…
Mi lacera tal vista.

RIGOLETTO
Tu sola resti al misero, ecc.

GILDA
If you are unwilling
to tell me about yourself…

RIGOLETTO *(interrupting)*
Never leave this house.

GILDA
I only go out to church.

RIGOLETTO
Oh, that is good.

GILDA
If you will tell me nothing of yourself,
let me know at least who my mother was.

RIGOLETTO
Oh, do not speak to your wretched
father of his lost love.
She felt, that angel,
pity for my sorrows.
I was alone, deformed, poor,
and she loved me out of compassion.
She died…may the earth rest lightly
upon that beloved head.
Only you are left to this wretch…
O God, I thank thee for that!

GILDA *(sobbing)*
What sorrow! What can have caused
such bitter tears?
Father, no more, calm down.
This sight tortures me.

RIGOLETTO
You only are left to this wretch. etc.

GILDA
li nome vostro ditemi,
il duoi che sì v'attrista.

RIGOLETTO
A che nomarmi? è inutile!
Padre ti sono, e basti.
Me forse al mondo temono,
d'alcuno ho forse gli asti.
Altri mi maledicono…

GILDA
Patria, parenti, amici
voi dunque non avete?

RIGOLETTO
Patria! parenti! amici!
Culto, famiglia, patria,
ii mio universo è in te!

GILDA
Ah, se può lieto rendervi,
gioia è la vita a me!

RIGOLETTO
Culto, famiglia, ecc.

GILDA
Già da tre lune son qui venuta
né la cittade ho ancor veduta;
se il concedete, farlo or potrei…

RIGOLETTO
Mai! mai! Uscita, dimmi, unqua sei?

GILDA
No.

GILDA
Tell me your name, tell me
what sorrow so afflicts you.

RIGOLETTO
What good would it do? None at all!
I am your father, let that suffice.
Perhaps some people fear me,
and some may even hate me.
Others curse me…

GILDA
Country, family, friends,
have you none of these?

RIGOLETTO
Country! family! friends!
My faith, my family, my country,
my whole world is in you!

GILDA
Ah, if I can make you happy.
then I shall be content!

RIGOLETTO
My faith, my family, etc.

GILDA
I have been here for three months now.
yet I have never seen the town:
if you would let me, now I could

RIGOLETTO
Never! Never! Tell me, have you been out?

GILDA
No.

RIGOLETTO
Guai!

GILDA *(da sé)*
Ah! Che dissi!

RIGOLETTO
Ben te ne guarda!
(da sé)
Potrien seguirla, rapirla ancora!
Qui d'un buffone si disonora
la figlia e se ne ride…Orror!
(forte)
Olà?

Giovanna comes out of the house.

GIOVANNA
Signor?

RIGOLETTO
Venendo mi vede alcuno?
Bada, di' il vero.

GIOVANNA
Oh, no, nessuno.

RIGOLETTO
Sta ben. La porta che dà al bastione
è sempre chiusa?

GIOVANNA
Ognor si sta.

RIGOLETTO
Bada, di' il ver.
Ah, veglia, o donna, questo fiore

RIGOLETTO
Woe betide you!

GILDA *(to herself)*
What have I said?

RIGOLETTO
Make sure you never do!
(to himself)
They could follow her, carry her off!
Here, the dishonouring of a jester's daughter
would be cause for laughter Oh, horror!
(aloud)
Hola?

GIOVANNA
Signor?

RIGOLETTO
Does anyone see me come in?
Mind you tell me the truth.

GIOVANNA
Ah no, no one.

RIGOLETTO
Good. Is the gate to the street
always kept locked?

GIOVANNA
Yes, always.

RIGOLETTO
Mind you tell me the truth.
O woman. watch over this flower

che a te puro confidai;
veglia, attenta, e non fia mai
che s'offuschi il suo candor.
Tu dei venti dal furore
ch'altri fiori hanno piegato.
lo difendi, e immacolato
lo ridona al genitor.

GILDA
Quanto affetto! quali cure!
Non temete, padre mio.
Lassù in cielo presso Dio
veglia un angiol protettor.
Da noi stoglie le sventure
di mia madre il priego santo;
non fia mai disvelto o franto
questo a voi diletto fior.

entrusted, pure, to your keeping;
be vigilant, that nothing may ever
sully its purity.
From the fury of the winds
that have broken other flowers,
protect her, and unstained
restore her to her father.

GILDA
What affection! What concern!
What do you fear, my father?
In heaven above, at God's right hand,
an angel watches over us.
We are shielded from all harm
by my mother's blessed prayers.
No hand will ever pluck or crush
this flower so dear to you.

The Duke, dressed as a commoner, appears in the street.

RIGOLETTO
Ah, veglia, o donna, questo fiore
che a te puro confi…
Alcun v'è fuori!

RIGOLETTO
O woman, watch over this flower,
entrusted pure, to your…
There is someone outside!

He opens the gate and, as he goes out into the street, the Duke slips into the court-yard and hides behind the tree, throwing a purse to Giovanna to ensure her silence.

GILDA
Cielo!
Sempre novel sospetto!

GILDA
Dear God!
Always some new suspicion!

RIGOLETTO *(a Giovanna tornando)*
Alla chiesa vi seguiva mai nessuno?

RIGOLETTO *(returning, to Giovanna)*
Has anyone ever followed you to church?

GIOVANNA
Mai.

GIOVANNA
Never.

DUCA *(da sé)*
Rigoletto!

DUKE *(to himself)*
Rigoletto!

RIGOLETTO
Se talor qui picchian,
guardatevi d'aprire…

RIGOLETTO
If anyone ever knocks,
mind you don't open the gate.

GIOVANNA
Nemmeno al Duca?

GIOVANNA
Not even for the Duke?

RIGOLETTO
Non che ad altri a lui.
Mia figlia, addio.

RIGOLETTO
Especially not for him.
My daughter, good night.

DUCA *(da sé)*
Sua figlia!

DUKE *(to himself)*
His daughter!

GILDA
Addio, mio padre.

GILDA
Good night, father.

RIGOLETTO
Ah! veglia, o donna, ecc.
Figlia, addio!

RIGOLETTO
O woman, watch over this flower, etc.
My daughter, good night!

GILDA
Oh, quanto affetto! ecc.
Mio padre, addio!

GILDA
What affection, etc.
Good night, father.

They embrace and Rigoletto departs closing the gate behind him; Gilda, Giovanna and the Duke remain in the courtyard.

GILDA
Giovanna, ho dei rimorsi…

GILDA
Giovanna, I am ashamed…

GIOVANNA
E perché mai?

GIOVANNA
Whatever for?

GILDA
Tacqui che un giovin
ne seguiva al tempio.

GIOVANNA
Perché ciò dirgli? L'odiate dunque
cotesto giovin, voi?

GILDA
No, no, ché troppo è bello
e spira amore.

GIOVANNA
E magnanimo sembra e gran signore.

GILDA
Signor né principe io lo vorrei;
sento che povero più l'amerei.

Sognando o vigile sempre lo chiamo,
e l'alma in estasi gli dice: t'a...

DUCA
(esce improvviso, fa cenno a Giovanna
d'andarsene, e inginocchiandosi ai piedi
di Gilda termina la frase)
T'amo!
T'amo; ripetilo sì caro accento:
un puro schiudimi ciel di contento!

GILDA
Giovanna? Ahi. rnisera! Non v'è più alcuno
che qui rispondarni! Oh Dio! nessuno?

DUCA
Son io coll'anima che ti rispondo.
Ah, due che s'amano son tutto un mondo!

GILDA
I said nothing of the youth
who followed us to church.

GIOVANNA
Why tell him? Do you dislike
this young man, then?

GILDA
No, no, he is too handsome
and I could be tempted to love him.

GIOVANNA
And he seems generous, a fine gentleman.

GILDA
I hope he's not a gentleman or a prince;
I think I should love him more if he were
poor.
Sleeping and waking, I call to him,
and my soul in ecstasy cries: I lo

DUKE
(rushing out and waving Giovanna away,
he kneels before Gilda and finishes the
sentence for her)
I love you!
I love you! Speak those dear words once more
and a heaven of joy will open before me!

GILDA
Giovanna? Alas! There is no one here
to answer me! Oh, God! No one?

DUKE
I am here, and my very soul answers you.
Ah. two who love are a world in themselves!

GILDA
Chi mai, chi giungere vi fece a me?

DUCA
Se angelo o dernone, che importa a te?
lo t'amo.

GILDA
Uscitene.

DUCA
Uscire!…adesso!…
Ora che accendene un fuoco istesso!
Ah, inseparabile d'amore il dio
stringeva, o vergine, tuo fato al mio!
È il sol dell'anima, la vita è amore,
sua voce è il palpito dei nostro core.
E fama e gloria, potenza e trono,
umane, fragili qui cose sono,
una pur avvene sola, divina:
È amor che agl'angioli più ne avvicina!
Adunque amiamoci, donna celeste;
d'invidia agli uomini sarò per te.

GILDA *(da sé)*
Ah, de' miei vergini sogni son queste
le voci tenere sì care a me! ecc.

DUCA
Amiamoci,
d'invidha agl'uomini sarò per te, ecc.
Che m'ami, deh, ripetimi.

GILDA
L'udiste.

GILDA
Who, whoever brought you here to me?

DUKE
Whether angel or devil, what does it matter?
I love you!

GILDA
Leave me.

DUKE
Leave you?…Now?…
Now that both of us burn with a single fire!
Ah, the god of love has bound
our destinies together, inseparably!
Love is the sunshine of the soul, 'tis life itself!
It's voice is the beating of our hearts.
Fame and glory, power and thrones,
are but fragile, earthbound things beside it.
One thing alone is unique, divine:
'tis love that bears us heavenwards!
So let us love, my angelwoman;
you would make me the envy of all mankind.

GILDA *(to herself)*
Ah, these are the tender, longed for words
I have heard in my maiden dreams! etc.

DUKE
Let us love, you would make me the envy
of all mankind, etc.
You love me, say it once again.

GILDA
You eavesdropped…

DUCA
Oh, me felice!

DUKE
How happy you've made me!

GILDA
Il nome vostro ditemi…
Saperlo a me non lice?

GILDA
Tell me your name…
Am I permitted to know it?

Ceprano and Bursa appear in the street below.

CEPRANO (*a Borsa*)
Il loco è qui.

CEPRANO (*to Borsa*)
This is the place.

DUCA (*pensando*)
Mi nomino…

DUKE (*racking his brains*)
My name is…

BORSA (*a Ceprano*)
Sta ben.

BORSA (*to Ceprano*)
Good.

He and Ceprano leave.

DUCA
Gualtier Maldè.
Studente sono, e povero…

DUKE
Walter Maldè.
I am a student, and poor…

GIOVANNA (*tornando spaventata*)
Rumor di passi è fuori!

GIOVANNA (*returning in a state of alarm*)
I can hear footsteps outside!

GILDA
Forse mio padre…

GILDA
My father, perhaps…

DUCA (*da sé*)
Ah. cogliere potessi il tradtore
che sì mi sturba!

DUKE (*to himself*)
Ah, if I should catch the traitor
who cost me such a chance!

GILDA
Adducilo
di qua al bastione…orite…

GILDA
Show him out
through the garden gate…Go now

DUCA	DUKE
Di', m'amerai tu?	Tell me, will you love me?

GILDA	GILDA
E voi?	And you?

DUCA	DUKE
L'intera vita…poi…	For the rest of my life…then…

GILDA	GILDA
Non più, non più…partite.	No more, no more…you must go.

TUTTÍE DUE
15 Addio! speranza ed anima
sol tu sarai per me.
Addio! vivrà immutabile
l'affetto mio per te.
Addio, ecc.

TOGETHER
Farewell…my heart and soul
are set on you alone.
Farewell…my love for you
will last for ever.
Farewell, etc.

He leaves, escorted by Giovanna. Gilda stands watching the gate through which he disappeared.

CD 1/Track 16   *Caro nome* is one of the most famous arias in Verdi's entire output and is frequently performed outside the context of the opera. It owes much to the "bel canto" style which dominates Verdi's early work, but the dreamy mood of a young woman in love is perfectly captured.

GILDA *(sola)*
Gualtier Maldè…nome di lui s'i amato,
ti scolpisci nel core innamorato!
Caro nome che il mio cor
festi primo palpitar,
le delizie dell'amor
mi déi sempre rammentar!
Coi pensier il mio desir
a te sempre volerà,

GILDA *(alone)*
Walter Maldè…name of the man I love,
be thou engraved upon my lovesick heart!
Beloved name, the first to move
the pulse of love within my heart,
thou shalt remind me ever
of the delights of love!
In my thoughts, my desire
will ever fly to thee,

e fin l'ultimo mio sospir,
caro nome, tuo sarà.
Col pensier, *ecc.*

and my last breath of life
shall be, beloved name, of thee.
In my thoughts, *etc.*

Taking a lantern, she walks up the steps to the terrace.

Gualtier MaIdè!

Walter Maldè!

Meanwhile, Marullo, Ceprano, Borsa and other courtiers have appeared in the road, armed and masked.

Caro nome, ecc.

Beloved name, etc.

BORSA
È là.

BORSA
There she is.

CEPRANO
Miratela.

CEPRANO
Look at her!

CORTIGIANI
Oh quanto è bella!

CHORUS
Oh, isn't she lovely!

MARULLO
Par fata od angioi.

MARULLO
She looks like a fairy or an angel.

CORTIGIANI
L'amante è quella
di Rigoletto.
Oh, quanto è bella!

CHORUS
So that's Rigoletto's
mistress!
Oh, isn't she lovely!

Gilda enters the house.

RIGOLETTO (*entrando concentrato; da sé*)
17 Riedo!…perché?

RIGOLETTO (*entering with a preoccupied air; to himself*)
I've come back!…Why?

BORSA
Slenzio. All'opra badate a me.

RIGOLETTO *(da sé)*
Ah, da quel vecchio fui maledetto!
(urta in Borsa)
Chi va là?

BORSA *(ai compagni)*
Tacete…c'è Rigoletto.

CEPRANO
Vittoria doppia! l'uccideremo.

BORSA
No, che domani più rideremo.

MARULLO
Or tutto aggiusto…

RIGOLETTO
Chi parla qua?

MARULLO
Ehi, Rigoletto?…DV?

RIGOLETTO
Chi va là?

MARULLO
Eh, non mangiarci!…Son…

RIGOLETTO
Chi?

BORSA
Silence. To work, now…do as I say.

RIGOLETTO *(to himself)*
Ah, I was cursed by that man!
(brushing against Borsa)
Who's there?

BORSA *(to his companions)*
Quiet…It's Rigoletto.

CEPRANO
A double victory! We'll kill him.

BORSA
No, tomorrow the jest will be even better.

MARULLO
Leave this to me…

RIGOLETTO
Who is that speaking?

MARULLO
Eh, Rigoletto? Is that you?

RIGOLETTO
Who is that?

MARUILLO
Eh, don't snap our heads off! This is…

RIGOLETTO
Who?

MARULLO
Marullo.

RIGOLETTO
In tanto buio lo sguardo è nullo.

MARULLO
Qui ne condusse ridevol cosa…
Torre a Ceprano vogliam la sposa.
Rigoletto (da sé)
Ahimè! respiro!
(a Marollo)
Ma come entrare?

MARULLO *(a Ceprano)*
La vostra chiave!
(a Rigoletto)
Non dubitare.
Non dee mancarci lo stratagemma…
(Gli dà la chiave avuta da Ceprano.)
Ecco la chiave.

RIGOLETTO *(palpando)*
Sento il suo stemma.
(da sé)
Ah, terror vano fu dunque il mio!
(a Marullo)
N'è là il palazzo. Con voi son io.

MARULLO
Siam mascherati…

RIGOLETTO
Ch'io pur mi mascheri;
a me una larva.

MARULLO
Marullo.

RIGOLETTO
It's so dark I can't see a thing.

MARULLO
We're here for a prank…
We're going to carry off Ceprano's wife.
Rigoletto (to himself)
Ah, I can breathe again!
(to Marullo)
How can you get in?

MARULLO *(to Ceprano)*
Your key!
(to Rigoletto)
Don't worry.
We've got it all arranged…
(giving him Ceprano's key)
Here is the key.

RIGOLETTO *(feeling them)*
I can feel his crest.
(to himself)
Ah, my terror was unfounded!
(aloud)
This is his place. I'm with you.

MARULLO
We're masked…

RIGOLETTO
Then I should be too.
Give me a mask.

MARULLO
Sì, Pronta è già.

MARULLO
Fine, it's right here.

He puts a mask on Rigoletto, at the same time blindfolding him with a handkerchief, then Positions him by a ladder which the others have leant against the terrace.

Terrai la scala.

You shall hold the ladder.

RIGOLETTO
Fitta è la tenebra.

RIGOLETTO
It's dark as pitch.

MARULLO
La benda cieco e sordo il fa.

MARULLO
The cloth has stopped his eyes and ears.

CORTIGIANI
18 Zitti, zitti, moviamo a vendetta;
ne sia colto or che meno l'aspetta.
Derisore sì audace e costante
a sua volta schernito sarà!
Cheti, cheti, rubiamgli l'amante
e al Corte doman riderà.

Cheti, cheti, ecc.
Derisore si audace, ecc.
Zitti, zitti, zitti, zitti,
cheti, cheti, cheti, cheti,
attenti all'opra, all'opra.

COURTIERS
Softly, softly, the trap is closing;
now we shall catch him, all unsuspecting.
The mocker so insolent, so unremitting,
will soon be a butt of derision himself!
Stealthily, stealthily we'll kidnap his mistress,
and in the morning the whole Court will laugh!
Stealthily. stealthily, etc.
The mocker so insolent, etc.
Softly, softly, softly, softly,
stealthily, stealthily, stealthily,
to work, to work.

Some of the men climb up to the terrace, force the door, open the gate from the inside to admit the others, then emerge dragging Gilda, gagged with a handkerchief. As she is carried off, she drops a scarf.

GILDA *(da lontano)*
Soccorso, padre mio!

GILDA *(from afar)*
Help, father!

CORTIGIANI *(da lontano)*
Vittoria!

GILDA *(più lontano)*
Aita!

RIGOLETTO
Non han finito ancor! qual
derisione!
(Si tocca gli occhi.)
Sono bendato!
Gilda! Gilda!

COURTIERS *(in the distance)*
Victory!

GILDA *(from further away)*
Help!

RIGOLETTO
They haven't finished yet!…A good joke
this!
(touching his eyes)
I'm blindfolded!
Gilda! Gilda!

He tears off the mask and the blindfold. By the light of a lantern left by Marullo's men, he sees Gilda's scarf, then the open gate. Rushing into the courtyard, he drags out the terrified Giovanna and stares at her, stupefied; speechless, he tears his hair. Finally, after a great struggle, he cries out:

Ah! la maledizione!

Ah, the curse!

He faints.

Act 2

A room in the ducal palace (There is a door on each side and a larger one at the far end flanked by full length portraits of the Duke and his wife. A highbacked chair stands near a velvetcovered table and other furniture.

CD 2/Tracks 1, 2 & 4

In this famous recitative, aria and cabaletta which introduce Act III, we find the Duke at his most sympathetic. Is this lecherous individual really capable of the kind of love expressed here?

DUCA *(entrando, agitato)*
Ella mi fu rapita! E quando, o
ciel?…
ne' brevi istanti, prima che il mio presagio
interno sull'orma corsa ancora mi
spingesse! Schiuso era l'uscio! la magion
deserta!
E dove ora sarà quell'angioi caro?
Colei che prima potè in questo core
destar la fiamma di costanti affetti?
Colei s'i pura, al cui modesto sguardo
quasi spinto a virtù talor mi credo!
Ella mi fu rapita! E chi l'ardiva? ma ne avrò
vendetta. Lo chiede il pianto della mia
diletta.
Parmi veder le lagrime scorrenti
da quel ciglio, quando fra il dubbio
e l'ansiadei subito periglio, dell'amor
nostro memore il suo Gualtier chiamò.

DUKE *(entering, agitated)*
She has been stolen from me! When, O
heaven?
In those few moments, before some
inner voice made me hastily retrace
my steps! The gate was open, the house
deserted!
And where is she now, that dear angel?
She who first kindled my heart with the
flame of a constant affection?
So pure that her modest demeanour almost
convinced me to lead a virtuous life!
She has been stolen from me! And
who dared do this? But I shall be
avenged.
The tears of my beloved demand it.
I seem to see the tears coursing from
her eyes as, bewildered and afraid at the
surprise attack, remembering our love,

Ned ei potea soccorrerti, cara fanciulla
amata; ei che vorria coll'anima farti
quaggiù beata; ci che le sfere agli angeliPer
te non invidiò.
Ei che le sfere, ecc.

she called her Walter's name. But he could
not defend you, sweet, beloved maid; he
who would pledge his very soul to bring
you happiness; he who, in loving you,
envied not even the angels.
He who, in loving you, etc.

Marullo, Ceprano, Borsa and other Courtiers enter.

BORSA, MARULLO, CEPRANO, CORTIGIANI
Duca, Duca!

BORSA, MARULLO, CEPRANO, COURTIERS
My lord, my lord!

DUCA
Ebben?

DUKE
What is it?

BORSA, MARULLO, CEPRANO, CORTIGIANI
L'amante fu rapita a Rigoletto.

BORSA, MARULLO, CEPRANO, COURTIERS
Rigoletto's mistress has been carried off.

DUCA
Come? E d'onde?

DUKE
What? From where?

BORSA, MARULLO, CEPRANO,CORTIGIANI
Dal suo tetto.

BORSA, MARULLO, CEPRANO,COURTIERS
From his house.

DUCA
Ah! Ah! dite, come fu?

DUKE
Ah! ah! Tell me, how was it done?

BORSA, MARULLO, CEPRANO,CORTIGIANI
Scorrendo uniti remota via,
brev'ora dopo caduto il dì,
come previsto ben s'era in pria,
rara beltà ci si scoprì.
Era l'amante di Rigoletto,
che vista appena si dileguò.
Già di rapirla s'avea il progetto,
quando il buffone ver noi spuntò;

BORSA, MARULLO, CEPRANO,COURTIERS
Together we went at nightfall,
to a street on the edge of the town;
there, as we had foreseen,
we found a most beautiful girl.
It was Rigoletto's paramour,
but as soon as we saw her, she vanished.
Our plans to abduct her were ready,
when along came the jester himself,

che di Ceprano noi la contessa
rapir volessimo, stolto, credè;
la scala, quindi, all'uopo messa,
bendato ei stesso ferma tenè.
La scala, quindi, ecc.
Salimmo, e rapidi la giovinetta
a noi riusciva quindi asportar.

DUCA (da sé)
Cielo!

BORSA, MARULLO, CEPRANO,CORTIGIANI
Quand'ei s'accorse della vendetta
restò scornato ad imprecar.

DUCA (da sé)
L dessa, la mia diletta!
(forte)
Ma dove or trovasi la poveretta?

BORSA, MARULLO, CEPRANO,CORTIGIANI
Fu da noi stessi addotta or qui.

DUCA (da sé)
Ah, tutto il ciel non mi rapì!

(alzandosi con gioia; da sé)
Possente amor mi chiama,
volar io deggio a lei:
il serto mio darei
per consolar quel cor.
Ah! sappia alfin chi l'ama,
conosca alfin chi sono,
apprenda ch'anco in trono
ha degli schiavi Amor.

whom we convinced, the simpleton,
that we were after Ceprano's countess.
So once we had set up the ladder,
he, blindfolded, held it secure.
So once we had set up the ladder, etc.
We climbed up and in less than no time
had carried the young girl away.

DUKE(to himself)
Heavens!

BORSA, MARULLO, CEPRANO,COURTIERS
When he realised how we'd paid him out,
you should have heard him curse!

DUKE(to himself)
Dear God! It's her, my beloved!
(aloud)
But where is the poor girl now?

BORSA, MARULLO, CEPRANO,COURTIERS
We brought her here ourselves.

DUKE(to himself)
Ah, heaven has not stolen everything from
me!
(springing up elatedly; to himself)
All-powerful love now calls me,
I must go to her at once:
I'd give my very crown to comfort that dear
heart.
Now she will learn who loves her,
she will find out who I am.
She must learn that even rulers can be
enslaved by love.

BORSA, MARULLO, CEPRANO, CORTIGIANI
Oh qual pensier or l'agita?
Come cangiò d'umor! ecc.

DUCA
Possente amor mi chiama, ecc.

He hurries away. Rigoletto enters, humming to himself and trying to disguise his grief.

BORSA, MARULLO, CEPRANO,COURTIERS
Oh, what makes him so excited? How his
mood has changed! etc.

DUKE
All-powerful love. etc,

CD 2/Track 5   The court falls silent as an anxious Rigoletto enters in search of his abducted daughter. In an attempt to mask his anguish he sings a carefree tune.

MARULLO
Povero Rigoletto!

RIGOLETTO
La rà, la rà, la rà, ecc.

CORTIGIANI
Ei vien…Silenzio.

RIGOLETTO
La rà, la rà, la rà, la rà, ecc.

BORSA, MARULLO, CEPRANO. CORTIGIANI
Oh, buon giorno, Rigoletto.

RIGOLETTO *(da sé)*
Han tutti fatto il colpo!

CEPRANO
Ch'hai di nuovo, buffon?

MARULLO
Poor Rigoletto!

RIGOLETTO
La ra, la ra, la ra, etc.

COURTIERS
Here he comes!…Be silent!

RIGOLETTO
La ra, la ra, la ra. la ra, etc.

BORSA, MARULLO, CEPRANO, COURTIERS
Good morning, Rigoletto.

RIGOLETTO *(to himself)*
They were all in on it!

CEPRANO
What news, jester?

RIGOLETTO
Ch'hai di nuovo, buffon? Che dell'usato
più noioso voi siete.

BORSA, MARULLO, CEPRANO, CORTIGIANI
Ah! ah! ah!

RIGOLETTO
La rà, la rà, la rà, ecc.
(spiando inquieto dovunque, da sé)
Ove l'avran nascosta?…

BORSA, MARULLO, CEPRANO, CORTIGIANI
(fra loro)
Guardate com'è inquieto!

RIGOLETTO
La rà, la rà, la rà, ecc.

BORSA, MARULLO, CEPRANO, CORTIGIANI
Sì! Guardate com'è inquieto!

RIGOLETTO *(a Marullo)*
Son felice che nulla a voi nuocesse
l'aria di questa notte…

MARULLO
Questa notte!

RIGOLETTO
Sì…Ah, fu il bel colpo!

MARULLO
S'ho dormito sempre!

RIGOLETTO
What news, jester? Only that you are more
of a bore than usual.

BORSA, MARULLO, CEPRANO, COURTIERS
Ha! ha! ha!

RIGOLETTO
La ra, la ra. la ra, etc.
(restlessly searching everywhere: to himself)
Where can they have hidden her?

BORSA, MARULLO, CEPRANO, COURTIERS
(aside)
See how upset he is!

RIGOLETTO
La ra, la ra, la ra, etc.

BORSA, MARULLO, CEPRANO, COURTIERS
Yes! See how upset he is!

RIGOLETTO *(to Marullo)*
I am glad that the cold air last night did
not harm you in the least…

MARULLO
Last night!…

RIGOLETTO
Yes! Ah, it was a fine trick!

MARULLO
But I was asleep all night!

RIGOLETTO
Ah, voi dormiste! Avrò dunque sognato!
La rà, la rà, la rà, ecc.

RIGOLETTO
Ah, you were asleep! So I dreamed it'
La ra, la ra, la ra, etc.

He moves off. Seeing a handkerchief on the table, he examines the monogram agitatedly.

CORTIGIANI *(fra loro)*
Ve' come tutto osserva!

COURTIERS *(aside)*
See how he inspects everything!

RIGOLETTO *(gettandolo; fra sé)*

Non è i I suo.
(forte)
Dorme il Duca tuttor?

RIGOLETTO *(throwing down the handkerchief; to himself)*
It isn't hers.
(aloud)
Is the Duke still asleep?

CORTIGIANI
S'i, dorme ancora.

COURTIERS
Yes, he is still asleep.

One of the Duchess's pages enters.

PAGGIO
Al suo sposo parlar vuoi la Duchessa.

PAGE
The Duchess wishes to speak to the Duke.

CEPRANO
Dorme.

CEPRANO
He's asleep.

PAGGIO
Qui or or con voi non era?

PAGE
Wasn't he here with you just now?

BORSA
é a caccia.

BORSA
He went hunting.

PAGGIO
Senza paggi! senz'armi!

PAGE
Without his escort! Unarmed!

CORTIGIANI
E non capisci
che per ora vedere non può alcuno?

ALL
Don't you understand that he can't see anyone right now?

RIGOLETTO *(che a parte è stato attentissimo
al dialogo, balzando improvviso tra loro
prorompe:)*
Ah, ell'è qui dunque! Ell'è coi Duca!

RIGOLETTO *(standing apart, he has followed the
conversation attentively, and now leaps among
them, crying out:)*
Ah, she is there, then! She is with the Duke!

CORTIGIANI
Chi?

COURTIERS
Who?

RIGOLETTO
La giovin che stanotte al mio tetto rapiste.
Ma la saprò riprender. Ella è là!

RIGOLETTO
The girl you carried off from my house last
night. But I shall get her back. She's in there!

CORTIGIANI
Se l'amante perdesti,
la ricerca altrove.

COURTIERS
If you've mislaid Your mistress, look for her
elsewhere.

RIGOLETTO
Io vo' mia figlia!

RIGOLETTO
I want my daughter!

CORTIGIANI
La sua figlia!

COURTIERS
His daughter!

CD 2/Track 6   *Cortigiani, vil razza dannata* is among the greatest arias in the repertoire. It begins with Rigoletto raging against the courtiers who have taken his
daughter, his anger supported by an insistent, turbulent figure in the strings.
When it is clear the courtiers will not let him enter the Duke's quarters, both he
and the orchestra dissolve into tears (01:09) and he is reduced to begging for
his daughter's return. It is a vocally and dramatically difficult tour-de-force for the
baritone and a real innovation in musical construction

RIGOLETTO

Sì, la mia figlia! d'una tal vittoria,
che? adesso non ridete?
Ella è là...la vogl'io...la renderete.

running towards the center door, but finding it barred by the Courtiers

Cortigiani, vil razza dannata,
per qual prezzo vendeste il mio bene?
A voi nulla per l'oro sconviene,
ma mia figlia è impagabil tesor.
La rendete...o, se pur disarmata,
questa man per voi fora cruenta;
nulla in terra più l'uomo paventa,
se dei figli difende l'onor.
Quella porta, assassini, m'aprite!

He again attacks the door, is dragged away from it by the Courtiers, struggles awhile, then gives up, exhausted.

La porta, la porta, assassini, m'aprite.
Ah! voi tutti a me contro venite!
Tutti contro me!
(piange)
Ah! Ebben, piango. Marullo, signore,
tu ch'hai l'alma gentil come il core,
dimmi tu dove l'hanno nascosta?
Marullo, signore, dimmi tu dove l'hanno
nascosta.
là...non è vero?...L là?...
non è vero?...è là?...non è vero?
Tu taci!...ohimè!
Miei signori, perdono, pietate!
Al vegliardo la figlia ridate!

RIGOLETTO

Yes, my daughter! After such a sweet
revenge, what? You're not laughing? She's in
there...I want her...Give her back.

Courtiers, vile, damnable rabble, how
much were you paid for my treasure?
There's nothing you won't do for money,
but my daughter is beyond any price.
Give her back or this hand, though
unarmed, will prove a dread weapon indeed.
A man will fear nothing on earth when
defending his children's honour. Assassins,
open that door!

The door, the door, assassins, open it.
Ah! You're all against me!
All against me!
(weeping)
Then I'll weep. Marullo, my lord, you
whose soul is as gentle as your heart, tell
me, where have they hidden her?
Marullo. my lord. tell me, where have they
hidden her?
She's in there isn't she? isn't that so?
in there? isn't that so?
You don't answer
Alas! My lords, forgive me, have pity!
Give an old man back his daughter!

Ridonarla a voi nulla ora costa,
tutto al mondo è tal figlia per me.
Signori, perdono, ecc.

To give her back can cost you nothing
now, but to me my daughter is everything.
Lords, forgive me, etc.

Gilda suddenly runs from the room on the left and throws herself into her
father's arms.

GILDA
Mio padre!

GILDA
Father!

RIGOLETTO
Dio! mia Gilda!
Signori, in essa è tutta la mia famiglia.
Non temer più nulla, angelo mio!
(ai Cortigiani)
Fu scherzo, non è vero?
Io, che pur piansi, or rido.
(a Gilda)
E tu a che piangi?

RIGOLETTO
Oh. God! My Gilda!
Sirs, she is all the family I have.
Don't be afraid now, my angel child
(to the Courtiers)
It was only a joke
wasn't it? I, though I wept before, now laugh.
(to Gilda)
Why do you still weep?

GILDA
Ah, l'onta, padre mio!

GILDA
The shame, father!

RIGOLETTO
Cielo! che dici?

RIGOLETTO
Good God! What do you mean?

GILDA
Arrossir voglio innanzi a voi soltanto…

GILDA
To you alone I confess…

RIGOLETTO *(ai Cortigiani)*
Ite di qua voi tutti!
Se il Duca vostro d'appressarsi osasse,
ch'ei non entri, gli dite, e ch'io ci sono.

RIGOLETTO *(to the Courtiers)*
Off with you, all of you! And if your Duke
should dare approach, tell him not to enter,
tell him I am here.

BORSA, MARULLO, CEPRANO, CORTIGIANI
(fra loro)
Coi fanciulli e co' dementi spesso giova il
simular; partiam pur, ma quel ch'ei tenti
non lasciamo d'osservar.

They go out.

RIGOLETTO
Parla…siam soli.

GILDA *(da sé)*
Ciel! dammi coraggio!
(a Rigoletto)
Tutte le feste al tempio
mentre pregava Iddio,
bello e fatale un giovine
offriasi al guardo mio…
Se i labbri nostri tacquero,
dagli occhi il cor parlò.
Furtivo fra le tenebre
sol ieri a me giungeva…
"Sono studente e povero",
commosso mi diceva,
e con ardente palpito
amor mi protestò.
Partì…il mio core aprivasi
a speme più gradita,
quando improvvisi apparvero
color che m'han rapita,
e a forza qui m'addussero
nell'ansia più crudel.

RIGOLETTO *(da sé)*
Ah! Solo per me l'infamia
a te chiedeva, o Dio…

BORSA, MARULLO, CEPRANO, COURTIERS
(among themselves)
With children and with madmen, pretense
is often best. We'll leave, but still keep
watch to see what he may do.

RIGOLETTO
Speak…we are alone.

GILDA *(to herself)*
O Heaven, give me courage!
(to Rigoletto)
Each holy day, in church,
as I prayed to God,
a fatally handsome young man
stood where I could see him…
Though our lips were silent,
our hearts spoke through our eyes.
Furtively, only last night he came to
meet me for the first time.
"I am a student and poor,"
he said so tenderly,
and with passionate fervour
told me of his love.
He went…my heart was rapt
in the sweetest dreams,
when suddenly the men broke in
who carried me away;
they brought me here by force,
cruelly afraid.

RIGOLETTO *(to himself)*
Ah! I asked infamy, O God,
only for myself,

ch'ella potesse ascendere
quanto caduto er'io.
Ah, presso dei patibolo
bisogna ben l'altare!
Ma tutto ora scompare,
l'altar si rovesciò!
(a Gilda)
Piangi, fanciulla, piangi…

GILDA
Padre!

RIGOLETTO
…scorrer fa il pianto sul mio cor.

GILDA
Padre, in voi parla un angioi
per me consolator, ecc.

RIGOLETTO
Piangi, fanciulla, ecc.
Compiuto pur quanto a fare mi resta,
lasciare potremo quest'aura funesta.

GILDA
Sì.

RIGOLETTO *(da sé)*
E tutto un sol giorno cangiare potè!

so that she might be raised
as high as I had fallen.
Ah, beside the gallows
one must raise an altar!
But all is now lost,
the altar is cast down!
(to Gilda)
Weep, my child, weep…

GILDA
Father!

RIGOLETTO
…and let your tears fall upon my breast.

GILDA
Father, an angel speaks through you and
consoles me, etc.

RIGOLETTO
Weep, my child, etc. When I have finished
what I must do here, we can leave this
house of doom.

GILDA
Yes.

RIGOLETTO *(to himself)*
A single day has changed everything!

Preceded by an usher, Count Monterone enters between two halberdiers and crosses the back of the room.

USCIERE *(alle guardie)*
Schiudete: ire al carcere Monteron dee.

USHER
Open up: Monterone is to go to the dungeon.

MONTERONE *(fermandosi verso il ritratto)*
Poiché fosti invano da me maledetto,
né un fulmine o un ferro
colpisce il tuo petto,
felice pur anco, o Duca, vivrai.

He goes out between the guards.

RIGOLETTO
No. vecchio, t'inganni…un vindice
avrai.
(Sì volge con impeto al ritratto.)
Sì, vendetta, tremenda vendetta
di quest'anima è solo desio.
Di punirti già l'ora s'affretta,
che fatale per te suonerà.
Come fulmin scagliato da Dio,
te colpire il buffone saprà.

GILDA
O mio padre, qual gioia feroce
balenarvi negli occhi vegg'io!

RIGOLETTO
Vendetta!

GILDA
Perdonate: a noi pure una voce
di perdono dal cielo verrà.

RIGOLETTO
Vendetta!

GILDA
Perdonate…

MONTERONE *(halting before the Duke's portrait)*
Since my curse has been in vain, and
neither steel nor thunderbolt has struck
your breast, you will live on, O Duke, in
happiness.

RIGOLETTO
No, old man, you're wrong…you shall be
avenged.
(passionately addressing the portrait)
Yes, revenge, terrible revenge is all that my
heart desires. The hour of your punishment
hastens on, that hour which will be your
last. Like a thunderbolt from the hand of
God, the jester's revenge shall strike you
down.

GILDA
O my father, what a fierce joy flashes in
your eyes!

RIGOLETTO
Revenge!

GILDA
Forgive him: and then we too may hear the
voice of pardon from Heaven.

RIGOLETTO
Revenge!

GILDA
Forgive him…

RIGOLETTO
No!

GILDA
Perdonate…

RIGOLETTO
No!

GILDA *(fra sé)*
Mi tradiva, pur l'amo; gran Dio,
per l'ingrato ti chiedo pietà!

RIGOLETTO
Come fulmin scagliato, ecc.

GILDA
Perdonate, ecc.

RIGOLETTO
No!

GILDA
Forgive him!

RIGOLETTO
No!

GILDA *(to herself)*
He betrayed me, yet I love him; great God,
I ask for pity on this faithless man!

RIGOLETTO
Like a thunderbolt, etc.

GILDA
Forgive him, etc.

Act 3

They leave through the main door.

The right bank of the River Minclo (On the left is a twostoried house, half fallen into ruin. At ground level, beyond an arcade, the interior of a rustic wineshop can be seen and a rough stone staircase leading to a loft with a small bed which, since there are no shutters, is in full view. Downstairs, in the wall facing the road, is a door that opens inwards. The wall itself is so full of cracks and holes here that whatever takes place within is clearly visible. In the background are the deserted fields along the Mincio, which runs behind a crumbling parapet. Beyond the river lies Mantua. It is night. Gilda and Rigoletto, both ill at ease, are standing in the road; Sparafucile is seated at a table in the wineshop.)

CD 2/Track 11   The final act begins with a brief, sorrowful prelude and Rigoletto asks his daughter once again, "Do you love him?" knowing the affirmative answer to come.

RIGOLETTO
E l'ami?

GILDA
Sempre.

RIGOLETTO
Pure tempo a guarirne t'ho lasciato.

GILDA
Io l'amo.

RIGOLETTO
And you love him?

GILDA
I always will.

RIGOLETTO
Yet I have given you time to forget.

GILDA
I love him.

RIGOLETTO
Povero cor di donna! Ah, il vile infame!
Ma ne avrai vendetta, o Gilda.

GILDA
Pietà, mio padre!

RIGOLETTO
E se tu certa fossi
ch'ei ti tradisse, l'ameresti ancora?

GILDA
Noi so, ma pur m'adora,

RIGOLETTO
Egli?

GILDA
sì.

RIGOLETTO
Ebben, osserva dunque.

He leads her to a crack in the wall.

GILDA
Un uomo vedo.

RIGOLETTO
Per poco attendi.

The Duke, wearing the uniform of a cavalry officer, enters the wine-shop through a door on the left.

GILDA *(trasalendo)*
Ah, padre mio!

RIGOLETTO
Poor woman's heart! Ah, the scoundrel! You shall be avenged, O Gilda.

GILDA
Have pity, My father!

RIGOLETTO
And if you were sure of his lack of faith, would you still love him?

GILDA
I do not know, but he adores me.

RIGOLETTO
He does?

GILDA
Yes.

RIGOLETTO
Well then, just watch.

GILDA
I see a man.

RIGOLETTO
Wait a moment.

GILDA *(startled)*
Ah, father!

DUCA *(a Sparafucile)*
Due cose e tosto…

SPARAFUCILE
Quali?

DUCA
Una stanza e dei vino!

RIGOLETTO
Son questi i suoi costumi!

SPARAFUCILE
Oh, il bel zerbino!

DUKE *(to Sparafucile)*
Two things and quickly…

SPARAFUCILE
What things?

DUKE
A room and a bottle of wine!

RIGOLETTO
These are the fellow's habits.

SPARAFUCILE
Oh, the gay blade!

He goes into an adjoining room.

CD 2/Track 12   *"La donna è mobile"* is one of the most well-known arias in all of opera.
Knowing he had a hit on his hands, Verdi withheld the tune from the leading
tenor until the day before the dress rehearsal.

DUCA
La donna è mobile
qual piuma al vento,
muta d'accento
e di pensier.
Sempre un amabile
leggiadro viso,
in pianto o in riso
è menzognero.
La donna è mobile, *ecc.*
é sempre misero
chi a lei s'affida,
chi le confida
mai cauto il cor!

DUKE
Women are as fickle
as feathers in the wind,
simple in speech,
and simple in mind.
Always the loveable,
sweet, laughing face,
but laughing or crying,
the face is false for sure.
Women are as fickle, *etc.*
If you rely on her
you will regret it,
and if you trust her
you are undone!

Pur mai non sentesi felice appieno chi su quel seno non liba amor! La donna è mobile, *ecc.*	Yet none can call himself fully contented who has not tasted love in her arms! Women are as fickle, *etc.*

Sparafucile returns with a bottle of wine and two glasses, which he puts on the table; then he strikes the ceiling twice with the pommel of his sword. At this signal, a buxom young woman in gypsy costume comes jumping down the stairs. The Duke runs to kiss her, but she eludes him. Meanwhile, Sparafucile, having slipped out into the road, speaks softly to Rigoletto.

SPARAFUCILE
é là il vostr'uomo. Viver dee o morire?

SPARAFUCILE
Your man's in there. Is he to live or die?

RIGOLETTO
Più tardi tornerò l'opra a compire.

RIGOLETTO
I'll come back later to conclude our business.

Sparafucile moves off behind the house in the direction of the river.

DUCA
Un d'i, se ben rammentomi,
o bella, t'incontrai…
Mi Piacque di te chiedere
e intesi che qui stai.
Or sappi che d'allora
sol te quest'alma adora.

DUKE
One day, if I remember rightly,
my pretty one, I met you…
I asked someone about you
and was told that you live here.
Let me say that ever since,
my heart has been yours alone.

GILDA *(da sé)*
Iniquo!

GILDA *(to herself)*
Deceiver!

MADDALENA
Ah! Ah!…e vent'altre appresso
le scorda forse adesso?

MADDALENA
Ah! Ah! And of twenty others
that maybe you're forgetting?

Ha un'aria il signorino
da vero libertino.

DUCA
Sì, un mostro son.

GILDA
Ah, padre mio!

MADDALENA
Lasciatemi, stordito!

DUCA
Ah, che fracasso!

MADDALENA
Stia saggio!

DUCA
E tu sii docile,
non farmi tanto, chiasso.
Ogni saggezza chiudesi
nel gaudio e nell'amore.
(Le prende la mano.)
La bella mano candida!

MADDALENA
Scherzate voi, signore.

DUCA
No, no.

MADDALENA
Son brutta.

DUCA
Abbracciami.

I think my fine young man
is a bit of a libertine.

DUKE
Yes, I'm a monster.

GILDA
Ah, father!

MADDALENA
Leave me alone, you scatterbrain!

DUKE
Ho, what a fuss!

MADDALENA
Behave yourself!

DUKE
Be nice to me.
Don't play hard to get.
Good behaviour doesn't exclude
jollity and love.
(caressing her hand)
Pretty white hand!

MADDALENA
You are joking, sir.

DUKE
No, no.

MADDALENA
I'm ugly.

DUKE
Kiss me.

GILDA *(da sé)*
Iniquo!

MADDALENA
Ebbro!

DUCA
D'amore ardente.

MADDALENA
Signor l'indifferente,
vi piace canzonar?

DUCA
No, no, ti vo' sposar…

MADDALENA
Ne voglio la parola.

DUCA *(ironico)*
Amabile figliuola!

RIGOLETTO *(a Gilda)*
E non ti basta ancor?

GILDA
Iniquo traditor! ecc.

MADDALENA
Ne voglio la parola! ecc.

DUCA
Amabile figliuola! ecc.

RIGOLETTO
E non ti basta ancor? *ecc.*

GILDA *(to herself)*
Deceiver!

MADDALENA
You're drunk!

DUKE
With love.

MADDALENA
My cynical friend, you like to joke, don't
you?

DUKE
No, no. I want to marry you

MADDALENA
I want your word of honour.

DUKE *(ironic)*
Sweet little maid!

RIGOLETTO *(to Gilda)*
Haven't you seen enough?

GILDA
The "wicked deceiver! etc.

MADDALENA
I want your word of honour! etc.

DUKE
Sweet little maid! etc.

RIGOLETTO
Haven't you seen enough? *etc.*

In this most famous quartet in the repertoire, Verdi manages to capture the mood of the Duke's seduction of Maddalena, her coquettish response and the anguish of Rigoletto and Gilda who observe the scene from outside.

Duca
Bella figlia dell'amore,
schiavo son dei vezzi tuoi;
con un detto sol tu puoi
le mie pene consolar.
Vieni e senti dei mio core
il frequente palpitar.
Con un detto, ecc.

Maddalena
Ah! ah! rido ben di core,
che tai baie costan poco…

Gilda
Ah, così parlar d'amore…

Maddalena
…quanto valga il vostro gioco,
mel credete, so apprezzar.

Gilda
…a me l'infame ho udito!

Rigoletto
Taci, il piangere non vale, ecc.

Gilda
Infelice cor tradito,
per angoscia non scoppiar.

Maddalena
Son avvezza, bel signore,

Duke
Fairest daughter of love,
I am a slave to your charms;
with but a single word you could
relieve my every pain.
Come, touch my breast and feel
how my heart is racing.
With but a single word, etc.

Maddalena
Ah! Ah! That really makes me laugh; talk
like that is cheap enough…

Gilda
Ah, these are the loving words…

Maddalena
…believe me, I know exactly what such
play-acting is worth!

Gilda
the scoundrel spoke once to me!

Rigoletto
Hush, weeping can do no good, etc.

Gilda
O wretched heart betrayed, do not break
for sorrow.

Maddalena
I, my fine sir, am quite accustomed

ad un simile scherzar,
mio bel signor!

DUCA
Con un detto sol tu puoi
consolar.

GILDA
Infelice cor tradito,
Per angoscia non scoppiar, ecc.

MADDALENA
Ah! Ah! Rido ben di core!
Che tai baie costan poco, ecc.

DUCA
Bella figlia dell'amore,
schiavo son de' vezzi tuoi, ecc.

RIGOLETTO
Ch'ei mentiva sei sicura.
Taci, e mia sarà la cura
la vendetta d'affrettar.
Pronta fia, sarà fatale,
io saprollo fulminar, ecc.
M'odi! Ritorna a casa.
Oro prendi, un destriero,
una veste viril che t'apprestai,
e per Verona parti.
Sarovvi io pur doman.

GILDA
Or venite…

RIGOLETTO
Impossibil.

to foolish jokes like this,
my fine sir!

DUKE
With but a single word you could relieve
my every pain.

GILDA
O wretched heart betrayed, do not break
for sorrow, etc.

MADDALENA
Ah! Ah! That really makes me laugh; talk
like that is cheap enough, etc.

DUKE
Fairest daughter of love, I am a slave to
your charms, etc.

RIGOLETTO
You are now convinced he was lying.
Hush, and leave it up to me
to hasten our revenge.
It will be quick, it will be deadly,
I know how to deal with him.
Listen to me, go home.
Take some money and a horse,
put on the menís clothes I provided,
then leave at once for Verona.
I shall meet you there tomorrow.

GILDA
Come with me now.

RIGOLETTO
It's impossible.

GILDA
Tremo.

RIGOLETTO
Va.

GILDA
I'm afraid.

RIGOLETTO
Go!

CD 2/Track 15　Verdi's creative genius is at it's zenith as the tension-filled plot unfolds against the backdrop of an approaching storm. We hear an aural representation of lightening, (00:54, 01:14), the sound of distant thunder, (01:15) and the sound of a howling wind produced by offstage men's chorus (01:19).

The Duke and Maddalena continue to laugh and talk together as they drink. Gilda having left, Rigoletto goes behind the house and returns with Sparafucile, counting out money into the cut-throat's hands.

Venti scudi hai tu detto? Eccone dieci,
e dopo l'opra il resto.
Ei qui rimane?

Twenty scudi, you said? Here are ten, and
the rest when the work is finished. He is
staying here?

SPARAFUCILE
Sì.

SPARAFUCILE
Yes.

RIGOLETTO
Alla mezzanotte ritornerò.

RIGOLETTO
At midnight I shall return.

SPARAFUCILE
Non cale:
a gettarlo nel fiume basto io solo.

SPARAFUCILE
No point: I can throw him in the river
without help.

RIGOLETTO
No, no; il vo' far io stesso.

RIGOLETTO
No. no, I want to do it myself.

SPARAFUCILE
Sia…il suo nome?

SPARAFUCILE
All right; his name?

RIGOLETTO
Vuoi sapere anche il mio?
Eglih è Delitto, Punizion son io.

He leaves; the sky darkens, lightning flashes.

SPARAFUCILE
La tempesta è vicina!
Più scura fia la notte.

DUCA
Maddalena?
(per prenderla)

MADDALENA *(sfuggendogli)*
Aspettate…mio fratello viene.

DUCA
Che importa?

MADDALENA
Tuona!

SPARAFUCILE *(entrando)*
E pioverà tra poco.

DUCA
Tanto meglio.
Tu dormirai in scuderia…
all'inferno…ove vorrai.

SPARAFUCILE
Oh, grazie.

MADDALENA *(piano al Duca.)*
Ah no!…partite.

RIGOLETTO
Do you want to know mine as well? He is
Crime, I am Punishment.

SPARAFUCILE
The storm is getting closer. The night will
be darker.

DUKE
Maddalena?
(trying to embrace her)

MADDALENA *(pushing him away)*
Wait…my brother is coming.

DUKE
So?

MADDALENA
Thunder!

SPARAFUCILE *(entering)*
It's going to rain soon.

DUKE
So much the better.
You can sleep in the stable…
or in hell…wherever you like.

SPARAFUCILE
Thank you.

MADDALENA *(softly to the Duke)*
Ah no!…You must leave.

DUCA (a Maddalena)
Con tal tempo?

SPARAFUCILE (piano a Maddalena)
Son venti scudi d'oro.
(al Duca)
Ben felice d'offrirvi la mia stanza.
Se a voi piace tosto a vederla andiamo.

Taking a lamp, he starts up the stairs.

DUCA
Ebben, sono con te…presto, vediamo.

He whispers something to Maddalena, then follows Sparafucile.

MADDALENA
Povero giovin!…grazioso tanto!
Dio! qual notte è questa!

DUCA (giunto al granaio, vedendone il balcone senza imposte.)
Si dorme all'aria aperta? Bene, bene.
Buona notte.

SPARAFUCILE
Signor, vi guardi Iddio.

DUCA
Breve sonno dormiam; stanco son io.

DUKE (to Maddalena)
In this weather?

SPARAFUCILE (softly to Maddalena)
It means twenty gold scudi.
(to the Duke)
I'll be glad to offer you my room. If you want to see it, let's go up now.

DUKE
Good; I'll be with you in a moment.

MADDALENA
Poor lad! He's so handsome! God! What a night this is!

DUKE (upstairs, noticing that the loft is open on one side)
We sleep in the open, eh? Good enough! Goodnight.

SPARAFUCILE
Sir, may God protect you.

DUKE
We'll not sleep long; but I'm tired,

He lays down his hat and sword and stretches out on the bed. Maddalena, meanwhile, has sat down at the table below. Sparafucile drinks from the bottle which the Duke left unfinished. Both are silent for a moment, lost in their thoughts.

La donna è mobile,
muta d'accento
e di pensiero…
muta d'accento
e di pen…
la donna…è mobil…ecc.
(s'addormenta)

MADDALENA
é amabile invero
cotal giovinotto.

SPARAFUCILE
Oh sì…ventiscudi
ne dà di prodotto.

MADDALENA
Sol venti!…son pochi!
valeva di più.

SPARAFUCILE
La spada, s'ei dorme,
va, portami giù.

Oh, women are fickle,
simple in speech
and simple in mind…
simple in speech
and in mind…
women…are fickle…etc.
(He falls asleep.)

MADDALENA
He is really most attractive,
this young man.

SPARAFUCILE
Oh, yes…to the tune
of twenty scudi.

MADDALENA
Only twenty!…That's not much! He was
worth more.

SPARAFUCILE
His sword: if he's asleep, bring it down to
me.

Maddalena goes upstairs and stands looking at the sleeping Duke, then she closes
the balcony as best she can and comes down carrying the sword. Gilda, meanwhile,
appears in the road wearing male attire, boots and spurs, and walks slowly towards
the inn where Sparafucile is still drinking. Frequent thunder and lightning

GILDA *(da sé)*
Ah, più non ragiono!
Amor mi trascina…
mio padre, perdono!
(tuono)
Qual notte d'orrore!
Gran Dio, che accadrà?

GILDA
Ah, my reason has left me!
Love draws me back…
Father, forgive me!
(thunder)
What a terrible night!
Great God, what will happen?

MADDALENA (*posata la spada dei Duca sulla tavola*)
Fratello?

GILDA (*osservando per la fessura*)
Chi parla?

SPARAFUCILE
(*frugando in un credenzone*)
Al diavol ten va!

MADDALENA
Somiglia un Apollo,
quel giovane, io l'amo,
ei m'ama…riposi…
né più l'uccidiamo.

GILDA (*ascoltando*)
Oh cielo!

SPARAFUCILE (*gettandole un sacco*)
Rattoppa quel sacco!

MADDALENA
Perché?

SPARAFUCILE
Entr'esso il tuo Apollo, sgozzato da me,
gettar dovrò al fiume.

GILDA
L'inferno qui vedo!

MADDALENA
Eppure il denaro salvarti scommetto
serbandolo in vita.

MADDALENA (*having put the Duke's sword on the table*)
Brother?

GILDA (*peeping through a crack*)
Who is speaking?

SPARAFUCILE
(*rummaging in a cupboard*)
Go to the devil!

MADDALENA
He's an Apollo,
that young man; I love him,
he loves me…let him be…
let's spare him.

GILDA (*listening*)
Dear God!

SPARAFUCILE (*throwing her a sack*)
Mend this sack!

MADDALENA
Why?

SPARAFUCILE
Because your Apollo, when I've cut his
throat, will wear it when I throw him in
the river.

GILDA
I see hell itself!

MADDALENA
But I reckon I can save you the money and
save his life as well.

SPARAFUCILE
Difficile il credo.

MADDALENA
M'ascolta…anzi facil ti svelo un progetto.
De' scudi già dieci dal gobbo ne avesti;
venire cogli altri più tardi il vedrai…
Uccidilo, e venti…

GILDA
Che sento!

MADDALENA
…allor ne avrai…

GILDA
Mio padre!

MADDALENA
…così tutto il prezzo goder si potrà.

SPARAFUCILE
Uccider quel gobbo! che diavol dicesti!
Un ladro son forse? Son forse un bandito?
Qual altro cliente da me fu tradito?
Mi paga quest'uomo, fedele m'avrà.

MADDALENA
Ah, grazia per esso!

SPARAFUCILE
L d'uopo ch'ei muoia.

MADDALENA
Fuggire il fo adesso.

SPARAFUCILE
Difficult, I think.

MADDALENA
Listen…my plan is simple.
You've had ten scudi from the hunchback;
he's coming later with the rest…
Kill him, and the twenty…

GILDA
What do I hear?

MADDALENA
…you've got…

GILDA
My father!

MADDALENA
…so we lose nothing.

SPARAFUCILE
Kill the hunchback? What the devil do you
mean? Am I a thief? Am I a bandit?
What client of mine has ever been cheated?
This man pays me, and I shall deliver.

MADDALENA
Ah, have mercy on him!

SPARAFUCILE
He must dic.

MADDALENA
I'll see he escapes in time.

She runs towards the stairs.

GILDA
Oh, buona figliuola!

GILDA
Oh, merciful girl!

SPARAFUCILE *(trattenendola)*
Gli scudi perdiamo.

SPARAFUCILE *(holding her back)*
We'd lose the money.

MADDALENA
L ver!

MADDALENA
That's true!

SPARAFUCILE
Lascia fare.

SPARAFUCILE
Don't interfere.

MADDALENA
Salvarlo dobbiamo.

MADDALENA
We must Save him.

SPARAFUCILE
Se pria ch'abbia il mezzo la notte toccato
alcuno qui giunga, per esso morrà.

SPARAFUCILE
If someone else comes here before midnight, they shall die in his place.

MADDALENA
é buia la notte, il ciel troppo irato,
nessuno a quest'ora da qui passerà.

MADDALENA
The night is dark, the weather too stormy;
no one will pass by here at this late hour.

GILDA
Oh, qual tentazione! morir per l'ingrato?
Morire!…e mio padre!…Oh cielo, pietà!

GILDA
Oh, what a temptation! To die for the ingrate?
To die! And my father?…Oh, Heaven, have mercy!

MADDALENA
é buia la notte, ecc.

MADDALENA
The night is dark, etc.

SPARAFUCILE
Se pria ch'abbia, ecc.

SPARAFUCILE
If someone else comes here, etc.

GILDA
Oh cielo, pietà, ecc.

GILDA
Oh, Heaven, have mercy. etc.

A distant clock chimes half-past eleven.

SPARAFUCILE
Ancor c'è mezz'ora.

SPARAFUCILE
There's still half an hour.

MADDALENA *(piangendo)*
Attendi, fratello…

MADDALENA *(weeping)*
Wait, brother…

GILDA
Che! piange tal donna! né a lui darò
aita!
Ah, s'egli al mio amore divenne rubello,
io vo"per la sua gettar la mia vita.

GILDA
What! A woman like that weeps, and I do
nothing to help him! Ah, even if he
betrayed my love I shall save his life with
my own!

She knocks on the door.

MADDALENA
Si picchia?

MADDALENA
A knock at the door?

SPARAFUCILE
Fu il vento.

SPARAFUCILE
It was the wind.

Gilda knocks again.

MADDALENA
Si picchia, ti dico.

MADDALENA
Someone's knocking. I tell you.

SPARAFUCILE
é strano!…Chi è?

SPARAFUCILE
How strange! Who's there?

GILDA
Pietà d'un mendico;
asil per la notte a lui concedete.

GILDA
Have pity on a beggar; grant him shelter
for the night.

MADDALENA
Fia lunga tal notte!

SPARAFUCILE
Alquanto attendete.

searching in the cupboard

MADDALENA
Su, spicciati, presto, fa l'opra compita:
anelo una vita con altra salvar.

SPARAFUCILE
Ebbene, son pronto; quell'uscio dischiudi,
più ch'altro gli scudi mi preme salvar.

GILDA *(da sé)*
Ah! presso alla morte, sì giovine sono!
Oh ciei, per quegl'empi ti chieggo
perdono!
Perdona tu, o padre, a quest'infelice!
Sia l'uomo felice ch'or vado a salvar.

MADDALENA
Spicciati, presto, ecc.

SPARAFUCILE
Bene, son pronto, ecc.

MADDALENA
Spicciati!

SPARAFUCILE
Apri!

MADDALENA
Entrate!

MADDALENA
A long night will it be!

SPARAFUCILE
Wait a moment.

MADDALENA
Come on, get on with it, finish the job. I
am eager to save one life with another.

SPARAFUCILE
So, I'm ready; open the door; all I want to
save is the gold.

GILDA *(to herself)*
Ah, death is near, and I am so young!
Oh, Heaven, for these sinners I ask thy
pardon.
Father, forgive your unhappy child! May
the man I am saving be happy.

MADDALENA
Get on with it, etc.

SPARAFUCILE
So, I am ready, etc.

MADDALENA
Get on with it!

SPARAFUCILE
Open up!

MADDALENA
Enter!

GILDA *(da sé)*
Dio! Loro perdonate!

MADDALENA, SPARAFUCILE
Entrate!

Dagger in hand, Sparafucile positions himself behind the door; Maddalena opens it, then runs to close the big door under the archway while Gilda enters. Sparafucile closes the door behind her and the rest is darkness and silence. Rigoletto comes down the road alone, wrapped in his cloak. The violence of the storm has abated, now there is only the occasional thunderclap and flash of lightning.

CD 2/Track 16   **(04:59)** As the storm unleashes its full-blown fury, Gilda falls under the assassin's knife and is placed in a sack for delivery to her unsuspecting father.

RIGOLETTO
Della vendetta alfin giunge l'istante!
Da trenta dì l'aspetto
di vivo sangue a lagrime piangendo,
sotto la larva dei buffon.
Quest'uscio….
(esaminando la casa)
è chiuso!…Ah, non è tempo ancor!
S'attenda.
Qual notte di mistero!
Una tempesta in cielo,
in terra un omicidio!
Oh, come invero qui grande mi sento!
(Suona mezzanotte.)
Mezzanotte!

SPARAFUCILE *(uscendo di casa)*
Chi è là?

RIGOLETTO *(per entrare)*
Son io.

GILDA *(to herself)*
God! Forgive them!

MADDALENA, SPARAFUCILE
Enter!

RIGOLETTO
At last the moment of vengeance is at hand!
For thirty days I have waited,
weeping tears of blood
behind my fool's mask.
This door…
(examining the house)
is closed!…ah, it is not yet time!
I shall wait. What a night of mystery!
A tempest above,
a murder below!
Oh, how big I feel now!
(The clock chimes twelve.)
Midnight!

SPARAFUCILE *(coming out of the house)*
Who's there?

RIGOLETTO *(about to enter)*
It is I.

SPARAFUCILE
Sostate.

He goes into the house and returns with the sack.

é qui spento il vostro'uomo.

RIGOLETTO
Oh gioial…un lumel.

SPARAFUCILE
Un lume?…No, il denaro.
(Rigoletto gli dà una borsa.)
Lesti all'onda il gettiam…

RIGOLETTO
No. basto io solo.

SPARAFUCILE
Come vi piace. Qui men atto è il sito.
Più avanti è più profondo il gorgo.
Presto, che alcun non vi sorprenda.
Buona notte.

He goes back into the house.

RIGOLETTO
Egli è là!…morto!
Oh sì…vorrei vederlo!
Ma che importa? è ben desso!
Ecco il suoi sproni!
Ora mi guarda, o mondo!
Quest'è un buffone, ed un potente è
questo!
Ei sta sotto ai miei piedi! E desso! 0 gioia!
é giunta alfine la tua vendetta. o duolo!

SPARAFUCILE
Wait.

He goes into the house and returns with the sack.

Here is your man, dead.

RIGOLETTO
Oh joy!…A light!

SPARAFUCILE
A light? No, the gold!
(Rigoletto gives him a purse.)
Let's throw him into the river quickly…

RIGOLETTO
No, I can do it alone.

SPARAFUCILE
As you wish. This is not a good place.
Further on the stream is deeper.
Quick, so that no one sees you.
Goodnight.

He goes back into the house.

RIGOLETTO
He's in there! Dead!
Oh, but I must see him!
But what's the use? It's him all right!
I can feel his spurs!
Now look upon me, O world!
Here is a buffoon, and this is a mighty
prince!
He lies at my feet! It's him! Oh joy!
At last you are avenged, O grief!

Sia l'onda a lui sepolcro,
un sacco il suo lenzuolo.
All'onda! All'onda!

Let the river be his tomb,
a sack his winding sheet! To the river! To
the river!

*He is about to drag the sack towards the river, when he hears, to his amazement,
the voice of the Duke in the distance.*

CD 2/Track 17   **(03:03)** From a distance, Rigoletto hears the Duke's flippant song. Horrified, he
wonders who is in the sack he carries. The drama of this moment is unprece-
dented in the annals of opera and a testament to Verdi's keen sense of the the-
ater.

DUCA
La donna è mobile, ecc.

DUKE
Women are as fickle, etc.

RIGOLETTO
Qualvoce!…illusion notturna è questa!
(trasalendo)
No!…No! egli è dosso…
(verso la casa)
Maledizione! Olà…dimon bandito!
(Taglia il sacco.)
18 Chi è mai. chi è qui in sua vece?
(lampeggia)
lo tremo…é umano corpo!
Mia figlia!…Dio!…mia figlia!
Ah no…è impossibil!
Per Verona è in via!
(inginocchiandosi)
Fu vision…é dessa!
0 mia Gilda: fanciulla, a me rispondi!
L'assassino mi svela…Olà?…Nessuno?
(Picchia disperatamente alla porta.)

RIGOLETTO
His voice!…This is a trick of the darkness!
(drawing back in terror)
No!…No! This is he!…
(shouting towards the house)
Damnation! Hola! You devil of a bandit!
(He cuts open the sack.)
Who can this be, here in his stead?
(lightning)
I tremble—It's a human body!
My daughter! O God! My daughter!
Ah, no, it cannot be!
She has left for Verona!
(kneeling)
It was a spectre It is she!
Oh, my Gilda, child, answer me!
Tell me the murderer's name! Is no one there?
(knocking desperately at the door)

Nessun!…
(tornando presso Gilda)
Mia figlia? Mia Gilda?…Oh, mia figlia!

GILDA
Chi mi chiama?

RIGOLETTO
Ella parla!…si muove!…
é viva!…oh Dio!
Ah, mio ben solo in terra…
Mi guarda…mi conosci…

GILDA
Ah, padre mio!

RIGOLETTO
Qual mistero!…Che fu?…
Sei tu ferita?…Dimmi…

GILDA *(indicando al core)*
L'acciar qui mi piagò.

RIGOLETTO
Chi t'ha colpita?

GILDA
V'ho ingannato…colpevole fui…
L'amai troppo…ora muoio per lui!

RIGOLETTO *(da sé)*
Dio tremendo! Ella stessa fu colta
dallo stral di mia giusta vendetta!
(a Gilda)
Angioi caro! mi guarda, m'ascolta!
Parla, parlami, figlia diletta.

No one!
(returning to Gilda)
My daughter? My Gilda? Oh.my daughter!

GILDA
Who calls me?

RIGOLETTO
She speaks!…She moves!…
She is alive! Oh, God!
Ah, my only joy on earth…look at
me…say who I am…

GILDA
Ah, my father!

RIGOLETTO
I'm mystified!…What happened?…
Are you wounded? Tell me…

GILDA *(pointing to her heart)*
The dagger wounded me here.

RIGOLETTO
Who struck you?

GILDA
I deceived you…I was guilty…I loved him
too much…now I die for him!

RIGOLETTO *(to himself)*
Great God in heaven! She was struck by
the bolt that I, in righteous vengeance,
loosed! (to Gilda) Beloved angel! Look at
me, listen to me! Speak, speak to me, dear-
est child.

(03:19) As Glide's life slips away, the orchestra sends her soul to heaven with the accompaniment of flute and high strings, growing softer and higher until she dies.

GILDA
Ah, ch'io taccia! a me, a lui perdonate.
Benedite alla figlia, o mio padre…
Lassù in cielo, vicina alla madre,
in eterno per voi pregherò.

RIGOLETTO
Non morire, mio tesoro, pietade!
Mia colomba, lasciarmi non déi!

GILDA
Lassù in cielo, ecc.

RIGOLETTO
Oh, mia figlia!
No, lasciarmi non déi, non morir.
Se t'involi. qui sol rimarrei.
Non morire, o qui teco morrò!

GILDA
Non più…a lui perdonate.
Mio padre…Addio!
Lassù in cicl, ccc.

RIGOLETTO
Oh mia figlia! O mia Gilda!
No, lasciarmi non déi, non morir!
(Gilda muore.)

GILDA
Let me be silent! Forgive me,
and him. Bless your daughter,
O my father—in heaven above, near my
mother, I shall pray for you evermore.

RIGOLETTO
Do not die, my treasure, have pity! Oh, my
dove, you must not leave me!

GILDA
In heaven above. etc.

RIGOLETTO
Oh my daughter!
No, you must not leave me, do not die.
If you go away, I shall be alone!
Do not die, or I shall die beside you!

GILDA
No more…Forgive him.
My father…Farewell!
In heaven above, etc.

RIGOLETTO
Oh my daughter, my Gilda! You must not
leave me, do not die!
(She dies.)

(06:08) Rigoletto recalls Monterone's curse one last time and the orchestra hurdles forward to the tragic closing chords.

RIGOLETTO
Gilda! mia Gilda!…L morta!
Ah, la maledizione!
(Strappandosi i capelli, cade sul
cadavere della figlia.)

RIGOLETTO
Gilda! My Gilda! She is dead!
Ah, the curse!
(Tearing his hair in anguish, he falls
senseless upon his daughter's body.)

END

Rigoletto

GIUSEPPE VERDI 1813–1901

LIBRETTO: FRANCESCO PIAVE AFTER VICTOR HUGO: LE ROI S'AMUSE

OPERA IN THREE ACTS

Gilda	Beverly Sills
Rigoletto	Sherrill Milnes
Il Duca di Mantua	Alfredo Kraus
Maddalena	Mignon Dunn
Sparafucile/Il Conte di Monterone	Samuel Ramey
Borsa	Dennis O'Neill
Marullo	John Rawnsley
Il Conte di Ceprano	Malcolm King
Giovanna	Ann Murray
La Contessa di Ceprano	Sally Burgess
Un paggio	Jennifer Smith
Un usciere	Alan Watt

Ambrosian Opera Chorus
Chorus Master: John McCarthy

Philharmonia Orchestra
conducted by   Julius Rudel

COMPACT DISC **1**   56.02

Atto Primo/Act One

|---|---|---|
☐1	Preludio	2.21
	(Orchestra)	
	Scena prima/SceneOne	
☐2	Della mia bella incognita borghese	1.47
	(Duca/Borsa)	
☐3	Quasta o quella	1.42
	(Duca)	
☐4	Partite? crudele!	1.33
	(Duca/Contessa Ceprano)	
☐5	In testa che avete	0.54
	(Rigoletto/Borsa/Coro)	
☐6	Gran nuova! Gran nuova!	
	(Marullo/Borsa/Coro/Duca/Ceprano/Rigoletto)	
☐7	Ch'io gli parli	3.20
	(Monterone/Duca/Borsa/Rigoletto/Marullo/Ceprano/Coro)	
☐8	O tu che la festa audace	1.27
	(Duca/Borsa/Rigoletto/Marullo/Ceprano/Coro)	

Atto Secondo/Act Two

☐9	Quel vecchio maledivami!	4.41
	(Rigoletto/Sparafucile)	
☐10	Pari siamo!	3.38
	(Rigoletto)	
☐11	Figlia!…Mio padre!…	6.36
☐12	Ah, veglia, o donna	5.27
	(Rigoletto/Gilda)	
☐13	Giovanna, ho dei rimorsi	2.42
	(Gilda/Giovanna/Duca)	

COMPACT DISC 2   63.03

Atto Secondo/Act Two